Yorkshire Folk in the Early 1900s:

my childhood in Mirfield

Joseph H Hird

Edited by Ruth Lesser

ISBN-13:978-1499557893
ISBN-10:1499557892

Cover photo: Joe and his mother (née Mary Brown), 1899

Also edited by Ruth Lesser:
The Snoring of a Thousand Men: Tales of Wartime Childhoods (Foreword by Fay Weldon), 2011, Newcastle U3A, NE1 5DW, UK.

When the War was over: Tales of a Mid-century World (Foreword by Jim Edwardson), 2012, Newcastle U3A, NE1 5DW, UK.

At Sea in the Great War as a 'Hostility Bastard' by Joseph H Hird, 2014.

Printed by CreateSpace in 12pt Garamond

In memory of Joe and Annie

CONTENTS

Editor's Note

A bulky red bag has lain below my bedroom window for several years. It contains blurred carbon copies of the painstakingly typed memoirs of my father, written when he was seventy.

It was the centenary in 2014 of the outbreak of World War 1 that made me search in the red bag for his memories as a seaman in that war. I learnt that his recall of that experience was insightful and astonishing in its clarity and detail.

As his Foreword explains, his motivation for writing was to tell his grandchildren (he had 17) of their heritage from that different world. I found myself enraptured by the resonance of life a hundred years ago and realised that his memories were worthy of a wider distribution. I wish I had been able to tell him how well written and compelling they are.

The oldest of my five children, Piers, has an excellent digital scanner, which enabled us to scan the fuzzy carbon copies in enough detail to make them possible to edit. The result was a first book "At Sea in the Great War as a 'Hostility Bastard' ", using my father's own words: unique, perhaps, amongst substantial historical records as the voice of a lowly sailor about his wartime years on the Lower Deck.

So I had to read more. There was enough in the red bag for another two books. Rich in variety and oddities, the present book is my father's account of his extended family and of his life in the Yorkshire village of Mirfield where he was brought up in a two-roomed back-to-back house a century ago.

Ruth Lesser (née Hird)

Joseph H Hird

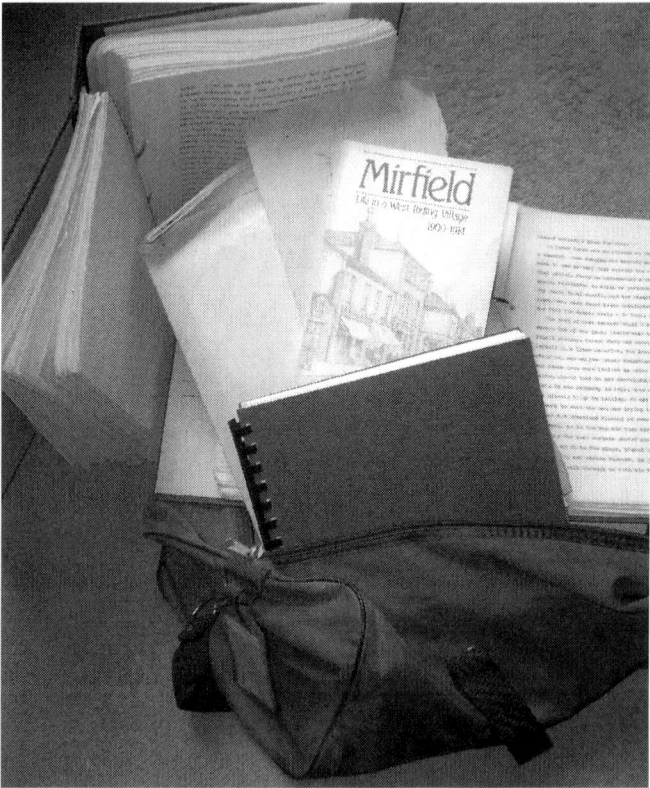

Foreword

Recently the teacher of grandson Tristram's class in his Primary School set as an exercise an attempt to build a genealogical table. The pupils were to ask at home about their family trees. Tristram wrote to me and, with the help of his grandmother Annie, it was possible to construct nets of names and relationships, wide but unfortunately reaching not far back. For this we must excuse our predecessors, whose narrow, practical, toilsome lives probably had no place for literacy. Before the Education Act of 1870 such children as had tuition received it at some school founded as a charity (and then aided, perhaps, by the Government grant) or at their parents' expense. Annie's mother was born nine years before the Education Act, her father seven years before, my father in the year of the Act and my mother four years later. It is not surprising that they did no private writing, except perhaps the rare, laboriously composed letter. As for my father's parents, I never heard of his mother reading or writing anything, and from his father the sole evidence was the signature 'John Hird' in a tattered little book on how to write a composition, which found its-way to the bottom of an untidy jumble of buttons, tape, string, pins, needles and knitting wool in a drawer at Mirfield. My mother's mother could neither read nor write. On a visit to her at Rydal Street, West Bowling, soon after I had begun to read, I stood by her chair to read something to her. She, listening, amused, then interrupted with: "You're makin' it up. Them marks doesn't say that!". My mother's father on the other hand, though I never heard of his writing anything, could read. He had had tuition. His father kept a public house off Manchester

Joseph H Hird

Road, Bradford, and, in the pre-1870 days and at a time when newspapers were expensive, men were attracted by the chance of hearing the news over their pints from someone who could read. When in the evening men began to come in, my great-grandfather called out "Jim! Come on lad" and Jim brought the newspaper into the tap-room.

Thus the genealogical tables sent to Tristram had width but not much depth. While making these tables I found myself adding little notes by the names and, at about that time, in the interval in a playing session with musical friends, I happened to refer to a custom of my early days and one of them said: "You ought to write that down". These stimuli, coming at a time when I must regard such writing as being 'now or never', perhaps as a pre-dotage effort, have led me to recall something of my early story and of what I remember of others connected with me or among whom I have lived. The periods and areas covered are limited. I have said little here about my secondary education, and I have hardly mentioned the war experience, the university, my teaching career, or personal history since leaving my parents' home. They are for another effort.

Apart from repetitions and the lack of good construction, two things have worried me. I have wondered whether my reminiscing has carried me into details which will probably interest no-one but me, and I have said hard things about my father. Without doing so I could not have accounted for my own experience, and in so doing I may have involuntarily given evidence to those most intimate with me as to how much of my father is in me. With much less excuse for me than there was for him, I plead as mitigation the disadvantage of early circumstantial limitations.

Joe Hird   January, 1968

1

My Parents and the Browns

Though I was an only child, my parents both came from large families. My father was one of six children living at Hill Top, Low Moor, Bradford. The family of eight lived in a low-decker, having one room with an alcove.

My mother's family of eleven children, the Browns, lived at (I think number 24) Balfour Street, Paley Road, East Bowling, Bradford. There were eight sons and three daughters, as well as an extra boy, a mate of one of my uncles. His name was Jim Wade. He needed a home, and my grandmother said they could fit him in; he was a quiet lad.

I was born there on the 11th of January, 1898. My first glimpses of the open air were when my mother took me into Bowling Park, and to St John's Church in Wakefield Road to be baptised.

My grandmother (Sarah Ann Brown née Britton) had long since ceased to go out to work, having been married at seventeen. She soon began to bear children, in all eleven survivors and two miscarriages. My mother said that her mother spent so much time in bed that she grew after she was married. She had, before her marriage to James Brown, worked in weaving and a trace of this experience remained in her language. In my childhood I used to be puzzled with a strange exclamation she made use of: "By t' mass!", to express pleasure or astonishment. I gathered long afterwards that she had picked this up from Irish weavers at work.

My Grandfather James Brown never came to see us, although he lived for six years after we moved to Mirfield.

My Grandmother Brown's much childbearing caused some dissatisfaction in my mother and her sister Martha, who had to work at home after a day's work in the mill. Baking was an almost daily task, particularly in the fetching of the flour and the kneading.

Mary and Martha Brown met Samuel Hird and Herbert Slater of Low Moor. Herbert was one of seven sons reared in a low-decker at Old Hill Top, Low Moor. (There were still Slaters there when I came to live in Low Moor in 1921; one son became publican at 'The Woodman' at Bankfoot, and I have sat by a Slater grandson in the choir at Holy Trinity Church, Low Moor).

My father, Samuel Hird, was at that time not in a comfortable situation. His father, John, had died when he was about six. My grandmother, Harriet Ann Hird, (née Horrocks, from Wyke) eked out a living by keeping a shop in her home, a low-decker at Portland Street. (I have the bin in which she kept her store of flour). She died in 1892, and was buried at Holy Trinity Church, Low Moor. The gravestone is quite legible still. The erection of this stone was a matter of pride and satisfaction on the part of my father as the other children were not willing to contribute to the expense.

The appearance of my Grandmother Hird is clear in my memory. There was a framed photograph of her above the place where my father sat, or rather lay back, in his chair in the evening with his feet on the oven except on baking nights, the oven being then too hot. A photograph of himself at his smartest was on the opposite side.

My father did not talk about his father, but he spoke with admiration of his mother, who used to kneel at her bedside and pray for the lads every night. She would say when my father was going out in his leisure times: "Whativver tha does, keep gooid coompany". He protested when she said this on the doorstep; he was ashamed of the neighbours hearing it.

My parents were married at Bradford Parish Church, as were Herbert Slater and my Aunt Martha. My cousin Bertha Slater (now Mrs Riley, widow, of Canterbury Avenue, Bradford) and I are both products of pre-marital matings. My parents married in July, and Bertha's in October, 1897. I was born on January 11th, and Bertha is eleven days younger.

My father was at that time in a determined mood. He and my Uncle Ben were left to fend for themselves in the house at Portland Street, and my father was anxious to have more home comfort. Grandmother Brown did not want my mother to leave home, where she was so useful, and my father was looked upon with disfavour. When my mother became pregnant there was a row between my grandmother and father, who clinched the matter by saying: "She belongs to me now!"

Joseph H Hird

I was born at my Grandmother Brown's in circumstances which were inevitably difficult amidst such congestion. My father obtained a small low-decker cottage on Hird Road, Low Moor. (The founders of the Low Moor Coal and Iron Company with headquarters nearby were Messrs Hird, Dawson and Hardy.)

At this time, 1898, my father was a striker, ie blacksmith's assistant, whose function was mainly to use the maul, a heavy hammer, while the blacksmith held the chisel or the punch on the red-hot iron with tongs and also to work the lever for the bellows. Previously, as a lad, he had had work in a mill, Cliff Mill, at Great Horton. I have heard him refer to 'roving' and 'bobbin-ligging'.

Some years before this the Low Moor Company had sunk its most far-flung pit at The Three Nuns at Mirfield (so called because it stood back in the fields at the bottom of a long, gentle slope leading down to the Calder River, and behind an old inn called The Three Nuns, adjacent to a Priory). My father, still a striker, was offered the post of blacksmith. This presented a problem. There would have to be a removal, and my mother was in weaving. It was decided to move, the command of a forge and an advance in wage being important considerations. He was to be paid, I believe, seventeen shillings and sixpence a week, and would have a striker as assistant. This man's name was Albert Daw. He had the misfortune to lose an eye from a flying fragment of iron while working with my father.

My father went first into lodgings with another pitman who had a low-decker at Cooper Bridge, near the 'Dumb Steeple'. In all, we lived in three houses in Low Moor. After the one in Hird Road we were in a house which my father called 'Meener House', belonging to someone known as

Yorkshire Folk in the Early 1900s

Meener Mounsey, and one in Collier Row, Common Road, Low Moor. Then a house was found at Kitson Hill, Battyeford, Mirfield. Our furniture was moved there from Low Moor by Brook Bottomley's brother, Zena, with his horse and cart. (Besides light-carting, he hawked yeast.) Brook was later to become my father-in law.

In the early days of our residence, there were a few visits from Bradford people, probably out of curiosity to see the place to which we had 'emigrated'. When young people married in those days it was usual to find a house near the parents. A former Bradford weaving friend of my mother's came one Sunday with her husband. My Grandmother Brown came with two of my uncles; my youngest uncle was only four years older than myself. My father's sister, Olive, came with some of her daughters, also on a Sunday. Such visits were not renewed. My father did not like visitors. Further contacts in reverse to Low Moor or Bowling were rare. So we settled into a detachment rarely interrupted by anyone who knew about our antecedents.

First rent was paid for this one-up-and-one-down cottage, at one corner of a square block of four, on 1st April, 1900. It was two shillings and threepence per week. We had one tap over a stone sink, no gas or electricity, **a** small cellar, a coalplace and a shared dry closet at the far end of the garden of the house behind ours.

In January 1901, as soon as I was three, I was taken to a house down Kitson Hill, where there were three children of Sam Copley and his wife. With these children I began to attend Battyeford Church Infants' School. I was boarded with the Copleys from Sunday night to Saturday dinner time for two shillings and sixpence.

During this time I saw nothing of my parents, except on one occasion when I caught measles and was wrapped up in a shawl, put over Sam Copley's shoulder and taken back up the hill to my house. My parents, though living only about fifty yards from the Copleys, did not initiate any contact. I never knew my father speak to the Copleys and the only occasion when my mother went was when she took me to introduce me. It gave me a queer feeling in those years from three to eight if I happened to see my mother outside when I was playing out on the hill.

Immediately she had left me with the Copleys my mother returned to work. This was now in a new area for her. She went first, on foot, to a mill called Hamer's, at Ravensthorpe near Dewsbury, nearly three miles away, and found some weaving. Later she transferred to a fine new mill, Learoyd's Trafalgar Mill, in Leeds Road, Huddersfield about four miles away. Trafalgar Mill was a short distance on our side of the Huddersfield Town football ground, and nearer still to what became with the war the British Dyeworks.

I lodged with the Copleys until I was eight, when they removed to Stocks Bank, taking a house next to the one found by Brook Bottomley in the following year, 1907, when he was transferred for work.

Occasionally I made contact again with the Copley children at their Stocks Bank house. There were now four, a daughter having been born while I was living with them at Kitson Hill.

Martha

After I went to live at Manor Row, Low Moor, (1921-1925), my Aunt Martha came to see us. On one occasion she told us about my mother coming with me to see her when I was one month old. My mother put me down on the sofa and said: "Look after 'im" and moved towards the door. Martha said "Where is ta gooin'?" -"To wark." In this way began that routine of work which lasted all through the time I lived at home.

As a baby I had the use of a cradle, but not for long. It was fetched for Minnie, my Aunt Olive's fifth daughter. I have reminded Minnie how I can prove that she is younger than I am, but not by much.

Martha had something about her. As a young girl she had had a session as a "Sunbeam" in the Christmas Pantomime in Bradford. The Sunbeams had to be of suitable size and shape and they performed as dancers and singers.

Martha continued to be proud of her voice and would sing at Christmas gatherings at my Grandmother Brown's. She could yodel; I heard this kind of singing for the first time. My Uncle Rufus and my Uncle Tom also sang sometimes before going out to the pub. Tom had a song about "What is the use of peeling an orange and throwing the inside away?"

Martha married Herbert Slater, my father's close companion. During all my time in the house at Kitson Hill, there was over the cellar door a framed photograph of Herbert and Sam in a sparring attitude with boxing gloves in Harold Park, Low Moor.

Martha was the next child after my mother, and the sisters were good companions. Bowling, where my grandparents Brown and their large family lived, was not far from Low Moor. It is not unlikely that the two young women met the two young men, Herbert and Sam, at one of the 'Tides', Bowling Tide or Carr Lane Tide (Low Moor) or Wibsey Fair. There seems to have been some hesitation in changing 2 & 2 into $(1+1)+(1+1)$. I remember my father taunting my mother during one of their terrible and frequent quarrels with "-- an' tha fancied 'erbert Slater!"

Joseph H Hird

Herbert was one of five brothers who formed a mining company. At one time they had a pit near the site of the present Odsal Stadium; at another they got coal near the windmill at Shelf, and finally at a site near the King's Road in Bradford. The work was hard and Herbert Slater caught a chill when sweating, and died of pneumonia. He would not break off working to take care of himself.

As a widow, Martha lived in a low-decker at Munster Street, Dudley Hill, and tried to make a little money by making pills. She could talk fluently and had a leaning for fortune-telling and herbalism. Later she lived in a waggon-caravan at Gain Lane, on the boundary of Bradford and Pudsey. It was of the same design as those which used to go round to the fairgrounds, but with the shafts removed. Her last private residence was at Undercliffe, in a cottage with one up and one down. She was very comfortable here, but ended her days in 'The Park', a Corporation Home for elderly infirm for whom no domestic assistance was available.

Rose Ann

Grandmother Brown's three daughters amongst her eleven children were in this order: my mother Mary (second child), Martha next, and Rose Ann, much further down the series.

When my mother and Martha got married, Rose Ann was too young to take their place adequately as domestic help. She was taller than her two sisters, and I remember her as cheerful and with a ready laugh in her voice.

She married a man called Barraclough and lived for a time in a street not far from her mother's, Rydal Street in West Bowling. All this area has recently been demolished as sub-standard. Later they moved to Keighley and had two sons, one called Lewis, after my Uncle Lewis.

Lewis Barraclough was killed riding a motor-cycle with his girl as passenger. His brother, whose name I have forgotten, promptly asked for his job as a fireman at a mill.

The father I remember from a photograph of him in khaki in World War 1, and as placid second fiddle to his cheerful wife on the rare occasions when we met.

Rose Ann died some years before her sisters. The last time I saw her was when she and Martha paid me a surprise visit at Carlton School at the close of afternoon school one day. There was no other reason for calling but their pleasure at seeing me again.

Rufus

As I have spoken of the three Brown sisters, I will take the brothers in order as nearly as I can. The first of the eight was Rufus, named after an uncle Rufus who was a soldier. After having served part of his time in India, that Rufus had died young from hard drinking and rough living.

My mother and Martha having come as numbers two and three, more brothers followed and, with two miscarriages and Rose Ann intervening, the series of male children continued till the eighth son arrived.

Rufus, like James his father, worked at Ripley's Dyeworks in Bowling, a firm still functioning. He followed the same pattern of living as his father. My grandfather and uncles who worked at Ripley's were pressers. The atmosphere of the room was hot, as I remember when I went with my Uncle Lewis to take supper in a pie-dish wrapped in a red handkerchief for my grandfather when he was on late shift. We were rewarded with a hot baked potato each. My grandfather wore a long brat.

Like his father also, Rufus was a frequenter of the pub, where Uncle Torn was popular as a singer. Rufus must have exercised more restraint or been tougher than his father. He was about seventy when he died, whereas Grandfather James Brown died aged fifty-two in 1906. I went with my mother upstairs at Rydal Street to see him. With sunken cheeks and mouth wide-open he was labouring hard for breath and having his lips moistened. While we were in the room my Great-aunt Ann came in, a white-haired upstanding woman, the oldest of the eighteen Brown children of that generation, my grandfather being the youngest. I was shocked to hear her say indignantly: "What 'as ta doon wi' thisen?". I have heard my Uncle Ernest tell how he went to The Prince of Wales pub (still there in Bowling) and sat down by my Grandfather James. The landlord said: "What's thine, lad?" Ernest answered : "Nought! I've come to fetch mi father." Ernest's opinion was that if his father had taken solid food with his beer he would have fared better.

Uncle Rufus married Clara. They had three children: my cousins Arthur, Florence Alice (Watmough) and Ada (Wolfenden).

During World War 1 I visited my Uncle Rufus and family when on leave from the Navy. They lived near the now demolished St Dunstan's Station not far from the centre of Bradford. The three children were all younger than me.

The last time I remember seeing Rufus was when he came over to Mirfield during the few days that my father's body lay upstairs waiting for the burial. My mother scolded him: "Tha nivver cooms to see us unless soomdi's deed!".

Yorkshire Folk in the Early 1900s

Rufus was a frequenter of a working men's club in East Bowling and a keen Labour man. His son Arthur has continued to live in the same area and to follow the same political interest, by this means becoming a City Councillor for East Bowling. He has a push and confidence similar to my Uncle Ernest's.

As a boy, my cousin Arthur wanted to spend all his time playing out at football. As a teacher I was to meet him after the war at Carlton High School where he was still a pupil, though never in my classes. His mind was still on sport and he left without taking School Certificate. He had various jobs, including attending to slot machines. He regretted having no qualifications but managed to get work in the Electricity Showrooms. He is designated on election notices as Managing Salesman and his style, as I find when I occasionally meet him, suits such a post. He is proud of his position on the Council, for whose meetings he gets time off his work. He has been on the Council many years but has been no higher than Vice-chairman of the Baths Committee. He was, for a time, on the Education Committee, being present at interviews for appointments. This is somewhat ironical, as he had rather despised school, not having enough patience with the contemptible teachers to want to take the exam.

By a further coincidence, Arthur's son, Kenneth, came to Carlton School. He also was not good at schooling, but got work as an electrician, constructing power stations up and down this country, and is now doing such work for a contracted period (having his family with him) at Bahrein.

Tom

Uncle Tom Brown volunteered for the South African War. I heard nothing of his experiences there, but he returned safely. He married and had two daughters, but was unsteady and his marriage was a failure.

From time to time he appeared at our house at Mirfield. He sat on the visitor's chair nearest the door, not often used, got a direct sermon from my mother, distant observation from my father, uneasy wonderment from me, a meal, a little money, and disappeared into the night, not having for a moment lost his patient equanimity.

When World War 1 came he was off again. His facility in roughing it and taking things as they came made the war seem no calamity to him, and he went with the first enthusiasts. Again he survived, fit and unscathed. On one occasion in a party of stretcher-bearers, he was the only man not hit when a shell mortally wounded all the others near him.

After my father's death, during the year when my mother remained in the house at Mirfield, he went to see her several times. She guessed he was wanting to settle there, but she stopped his visits, saying a wrong interpretation might be put upon them by the neighbours. Having no regular work he took to the road, remaining, in spite of this, healthy and cheerful.

However, he had a stroke of luck at the end. His daughters got married, one of them going to live at Birkdale, near Southport. She became curious about the whereabouts of her father and put an enquiry in the newspapers. Tom had remained in the Bradford area, lodging somewhere in Manningham. Someone who knew him drew his attention to the newspaper and he went to Birkdale, with what result I do not know.

I last saw him at my Grandmother Brown's funeral. At the tea at Saint Oswald's Church in Little Horton he was a healthy-looking, cheerful man, now grey-haired, but still mysteriously vague. He maintained his toughness and alcoholic sociability long after that.

The last thing I heard of him before the news from Birkdale was a mention by my Uncle Ernest that Tom had been 'had up' for drunkenness.

Ernest

Ernest was the uncle I saw most frequently in his later years. I had first seen him when he called for a short time with his wife Dora during the Christmas gatherings at my Grandmother Brown's. Dora was rather delicate and had a leaning towards refinement. When we left Shelf in January 1932 to live in Horton Grange Road, Bradford, she came from their house and shop in Saint Margaret's Road nearby, to sit in our garden and talk for a while.

Dora and Ernest were girl and boy sweethearts. When he had any money for a little indulgence he shared equally. My mother told me how he would count the number of sweets in a bag and divide by two. There had been a child, still-born. Ernest took an interest in his wife's sister's son, encouraging him to get education and qualifications, but fruitlessly. Later, Ernest helped my cousin Ada Wolfenden's son (grandson of Rufus) through divorce proceedings.

Ernest almost died of an illness as a boy when the family lived at Eccleshill. My mother said he was baptised at Eccleshill Church, but he recovered to become a vigorous, ambitious young man. He would tell me in more recent years that part of his regret about my Grandfather Brown's visits to The Prince of Wales was that, out of the £10 wage sometimes achieved, a good deal could have been done to set up those lads.

Joseph H Hird

Ernest believed that his vocation was to have been a lawyer. He loved to impart emphatically the fruits of his wisdom and experience as a businessman. I have often met him in the street, as my usual walk to town took me past his shop and the entry where he garaged his car and had his workshop and display-room. He never wanted to know anything about what I was thinking or doing or about my family. When I tried to tell him he soon moved the talk back to himself. During the years when my mother came to live near us he seldom came to see her. His pride in himself did not find easy expression in her presence.

His ambition as a lad found a channel for progress in engineering. No capital was required and he was soon self-supporting. He went through his apprenticeship and became a qualified engineer. This was useful when the war came. It did not satisfy his ambition, however. After the war, my Uncle Arthur Brown, who had made good in the United States, persuaded Ernest to try his luck there also, but it did not take him long to come to the conclusion that there was no more scope for him there than he could find in England. He came back to plan to be his own master.

He and Dora lived in Barlow Road, off Spencer Road, and he began to sell carpets and furniture, using a bedroom as salesroom. For this business he needed credit and tried to get it from Firth's of Bailiff Bridge, a company of high standing. He was disappointed. He heard that enquiries had been made, and Firth's knew about the bedroom and the merely part-time business. He had to make a decision, to be an employee in engineering, or a master in furnishing.

He told me that essentials for such a business were a motor-car and a telephone, to be followed by a showroom. He took the shop at the junction of St

Yorkshire Folk in the Early 1900s

Margaret's Road and Woodhead Road (now selling newspapers and sweets) and used the front room for display, as well as one bedroom. Later he acquired a showroom in a Working Men's Club nearby. Under the showroom he had his workshop, used mainly for repairing chairs. The Club was useful. Ernest was a member (one of the conditions of the lease) and found it very convenient to be able to break off work for his morning glass of Guinness, while hobnobbing with a view to widening his custom. He extended this method by joining the Lidget Green Conservative Club and the Lidget Green Liberal Club as well as the Freemasons. He tried to impress me with the mysteries of this organisation and his success in getting big orders from gentlemen of standing.

During the Second World War Ernest got several contracts for blacking out large buildings, one being a hall (now a school at Cottingley) and I tried to get the contract for Carlton School for him when I was teaching there.

He was now as high up as he, a lawyer manqué, could get. He was proud of being able to get carpets on credit up to the value of £2000, and of the business scoops he had made.

In the hairdresser's one day he met another man who had set up in business down Woodhead Road (*Essonia*, flavouring and colouring for soft drinks), and in a casual conversation they arranged to go together on a cruise to the Canary Islands and South America. In his account of the cruise there was little about what happened outside the ship except that it was warm and traffic conditions were bad in South America. In the ship he had met many wealthy and important people (some of them titled) with whom he discussed commercial matters.

Dora died and Ernest married a widow of fifty with a daughter. He moved out of the shop to live in his wife's house in Rugby Place but kept on the furnishing business from the workshop. He eventually gave the business to an assistant who had worked for him for many years, continuing himself to help in getting business and in the transport of carpets with his car, of which he had become very fond. He told me that if he had to stop motoring he would not have much to live for. They did a little touring, in this country and in Scotland. Meeting new people on his travels suited Ernest's temperament and replenished his fund of talk.

Ernest never visited us at Mirfield, nor did my mother ever go to see him. My father had been rude to him at one of the rare meetings at Christmas at my grandmother's. Ernest did not conceal his pride in his rise to a collar and tie job and being his own master. My father tried to deflate him: "Tha thinks tha art soomdi na!" There may have been some envy in this. My father had not moved up out of the dirt of the pit where he had been since 1900.

I got on well with Ernest in the period after we came to live near him, soon learning that all I was required to do at our casual meetings in the road was to listen during the time he could spare before Guinness time, or dinner time, or before his next little business trip. I often saw the car standing by the house (his wife's). He took to golf, this being his latest spread of the net for contacts, and played on Baildon Moor while his wife, who developed a falling sickness, sat in the car.

In his later years also he invested in sport, buying half a dog at the Bradford City Dog-racing Stadium. The fortunes of his thoroughbred dropped out of his conversation; the punters there were not likely to have much time or inclination to talk about carpets and curtains, and the track itself went out of business some years later.

I was considered to have 'moved up' in becoming a teacher. All my relations had this idea. Up to Ernest's achievement none had had jobs where the same suit could be worn on weekdays as on Sundays. Ernest was on the look-out to moderate any satisfaction I might have had, but I was ready to meet him more than half-way, by pointing out how much more favourable the social system was for me in my early days than it had been for him, as well as referring to my more favourable family circumstances. We could exercise a certain amount of tact.

He met me when I was at St Columba's Church as verger in 1949, where I worked outside sometimes, clearing out the ashes, getting in coke, cleaning the windows and cutting the grass. There was no change in his attitude to me or in the themes of his conversation.

Ernest reached his seventies. He became ill with a stoppage in the bowels and returned home after a period in hospital with instructions to return for regular examination. Unexpectedly he was detained after one of these and soon died. I went to his funeral, meeting Rufus's daughter, Florence Alice Watmough, at the house in Rugby Place. She and I were the ones on the Brown side, except for a man whose identity came as a surprise to me.

James

I recognised the Brown face, and the man turned out to be my Uncle James, whom I recall seeing on only one occasion before. During my boyhood he was a soldier in India. At Mirfield in the bedroom there was a framed photograph of him sitting up very smartly as a cavalryman on horseback. He was stationed at Madras. There was a story that on a mission into the interior the natives liked him so much that they wanted him to stay with them. The importance of the photograph was partly in the frame which my father had made himself.

I first saw James at my Grandmother Brown's when my mother took me on a visit. He had finished his time in the army and was sitting near the oven with a shawl over his shoulders, feeling the cold after southern India. In later years my Uncle Ernest told me about an angry woman coming to the door in Rugby Place, wanting Ernest to tell her where James was. She was James's wife. She did not get the necessary information.

At Ernest's funeral I should have liked to hear more about James' history, but there was little opportunity. Like Tom he had weathered life's irregularities, and was now open-faced, fat and cheerful. Only three personal details came out; he was lodging in Lime Street (only a quarter of a mile away); he tried to compare his age with my Uncle Arthur's; India had done him a lot of good. Florence and I could have told him a good deal about family history, but he showed no interest.

Nearly all my mother' s brothers learnt to jog along in their way. So far as I know I have never seen James since.

Arthur

Arthur is one of the most interesting of my mother's brothers. Starting work in Bradford at Ripley's Dyeworks, according to the now established pattern, he found it not to his liking. He joined the Regular Army at Halifax, but in an even shorter time he found the rough life distasteful. He wanted to get out but had no money. Walking from Halifax to Mirfield one Saturday, he came to ask my father to lend him the necessary £5. This was not a smooth negotiation. It happened that my father had decided to go to Brighouse, three miles away, to buy a bird-cage for our canary. Arthur had to walk there with the three of us. He got his money and walked back to Halifax. During the whole time he had been patient and quietly pliant under my father's mood. That was in 1906. I was eight. I remember Arthur's red coat and the feeling of apprehension about the result of his visit.

He got out of the army, probably fortunately, for by the time the First World War came he would have been a thoroughly trained soldier of about twenty-six years of age.

Somehow he scraped together enough money to go steerage from Liverpool to America. The voyage was unpleasant, among rough, dirty men speaking various languages. Arthur never moved far from the eastern side of the States. He did any casual work he could get in order to stay alive. Attending evening classes in engineering draughtsmanship, he obtained a certificate and was able to get work at the drawing-board. After a period at Utica in New York State he settled in Providence, Rhode Island. He got work with the engineering firm of Brown Sharp's and was now standing firmly on his own feet.

In 1912 he could afford to come over to Europe on a visit. He turned up at our house one baking-night, smart, cheerful and at ease. He spent the evening with us, straightened up about the debt, and departed. He had already been to Paris.

I started a correspondence with him and up till recently have never lost touch, though now news comes on a Christmas card from Sylvia, his daughter-in-law. Arthur's success and the romantic opportunities of the States were shown on a photograph he had sent us. Arthur was to be seen with hunting dress, broad-brimmed hat and gun on the far side of a pool in forest land.

The intimacy and small range of social life in our village was shown by the arrival on one occasion of a letter returned from the United States. It had not found Arthur and it came back addressed by the Post Office to Joseph Henry, Kitson Hill, Mirfield. There were no numbers on the houses then, and there was no one in that area who did not know me by my Christian names.

On that visit in 1912 he told us he was going to get married on his return. At a Methodist Chapel where he had gone to make social contact, he had met Laura of a family emigrated from Birmingham. Their son, my cousin Arthur Howard Brown, was born in 1913. In 1916 Arthur, with Laura and the little toddler, was back in England, as a draughtsman at David Brown's in Huddersfield, a firm which is now world-famous. A house to rent had been found at Birkby, a former tenant having been Wagstaff, a household name in Rugby football. The United States was not in the war at that time and engineering had, of course, become intensely active in this country. We paid a visit for a Saturday tea at Birkby. Arthur was a competent host and Laura an acquiescent second fiddle to him. Such an occasion was not comfortable. My father was not accustomed to visiting. It would have been a good opportunity for hearing fully about life in the States, but my father had no ideas for giving the right cues and could not reconcile himself to being a listener. He abruptly wanted to know about practical matters such as wage and rent, and was obviously aware that his usual way of wolfish attack on the food would be inappropriate. He had seen Arthur as a mere lad and later as a supplicant for £5, and this ease and success aroused his envy. His comment on Laura when we returned home was:"She seems ta 'a nought special

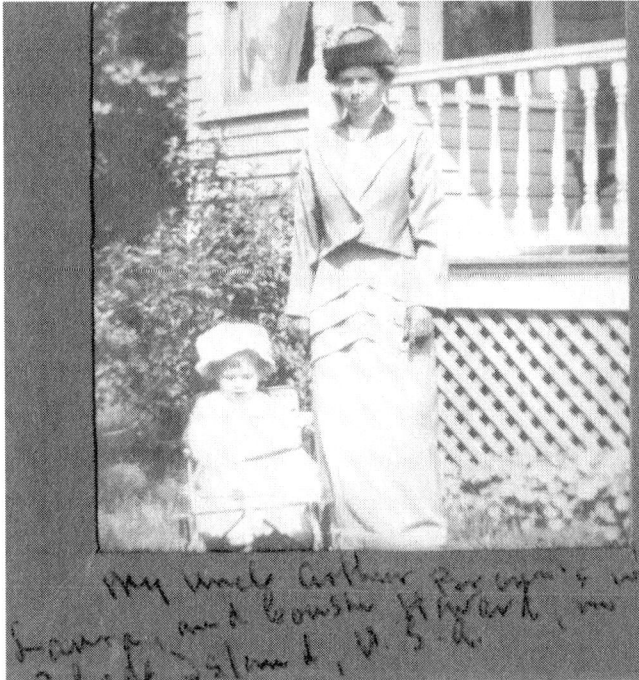

My uncle Arthur Rogson's wi Laura and cousin Howard, on Long Island, U.S.A.

abaht 'er." My mother would have taken pleasure in the visit. She admired the way in which Arthur had pulled through.

There was no return visit to our house, but I went alone to Birkby. I remember the confusion I felt at the mess I made when Arthur suggested I should make a cigarette with the paper and tobacco he supplied. He showed me the blueprint of drawings he had made of gears and an article of his which had been published in a technical magazine.

He did not stay long in England. After the intermediate step of the Derby Scheme for volunteering for war service (a small payment and an armlet received, and registration), conscription was approaching, and Arthur did not wish to be involved in our war. He may have been mistaken about this. A large number of able-bodied men engaged in essential production did not go to the fighting. He wished to be fully an American citizen, and decided to go back to Brown Sharp's in Providence. In the slump of the late twenties Arthur tried to make a living as a coal

merchant, but after a time returned to his proper work as a draughtsman. He was able to finish his working career in comfort, enjoying the runs down to the sea at Narragansett Bay and, after retirement, to Miami. There he remained until recently. Sylvia, Howard's wife, said on her Christmas card of 1966 that it had been necessary to bring the old folks nearer to Adams, Massachusetts. After the return to the USA Arthur and Laura's second son Gordon had been born. Both the boys did well. Arthur sent us a photograph of Howard holding his certificate of 'graduation' from High School. (*The photograph shows Howard on the left, with his younger brother Gordon and parents at their house in Rhode Island.*)

Yorkshire Folk in the Early 1900s

Long afterwards the Second World War brought Howard to Europe. He came twice to see us, unfortunately missing by about a month seeing my mother, who had died in April, 1944. We lived then at 7 Estcourt Grove, and the nearby house at 9 Estcourt Road, where my mother had moved to some months after my father's death, was still in my possession. Howard was comfortably accommodated there. Two details struck me. In coming from the station in Bradford, he had disdained the convenient public transport and engaged a taxi. The other was his way of eating dinner with a fork only and of committing the offence of leaving some of it on the plate. We enjoyed his brief stay. We were able to make a little comparison with American schooling My son Brian showed Howard a mathematics test paper from school. He was quite nonplussed.

In 1946 Howard came again to see us. The war was now over and he had moved up from the rank of Lieutenant in the Air Force to Captain. He had flown over from Germany. His work had been in the system of control of air attacks. He told us a few unpleasant things in the behaviour towards the defeated side. In the move forward into Germany the invaders went into houses and said: "Out in five minutes!". There was much looting, and an order was issued about it. The commander of Howard's group read out the order with a grin on his face. The men knew how much looting he had done himself. On another occasion an ambulance bringing American wounded was being unloaded when a bearer tripped and the wounded man was tipped off. The comical sight caused an outburst of laughter among German prisoners present. A guard opened fire on them with his sub-machine gun.

Joseph H Hird

Howard returned to the United States and bought a laundry business at Adams, Massachusetts, not difficult of access from Providence. He became prominent in the Lions organisation.

His brother Gordon entered the Air Arm of the United States Fleet. This work took him away from home. We have heard of him being at Corpus Christi in Texas, and when we heard last he was working in the Pentagon. During the second World War he was decorated for leading an air attack on Japan, and he has had a tour of duty there. After the war we received a copy of an account of the commissioning of a new aircraft carrier. It was such a vast concern that it had several departmental captains. Gordon's photograph appeared among these.

Herbert

The oldest of the last three brothers was Uncle Herbert. When we first met I remember him as the big boy amongst us. My first particular memory of him is of a visit he paid to Kitson Hill when he had broken his arm and of his skill in drawing with the other hand. He also came once on his bicycle and took home, fastened on his back, a stool given as a present. My father brought several stools of this type from his work at the Three Nuns Pit.

I was at home alone in the holidays on one occasion when Herbert suddenly appeared at our house with a young woman. He seemed jolly and sent me out to buy some sweets. The couple did not remain till my parents came home from work. Herbert did not marry this young woman. He had an illegitimate son in

28

whom he maintained an interest. I heard of his saving up to buy a bicycle for him.

On leaving school Herbert went to work as a packer at the firm of Buckle Crossley's, dyers, in Lidget Green. He was interested in machines, and when the war came he went for engineering training. He got into the Royal Engineers, his work being to take to Birmingham motor vehicles which had been damaged in France. He liked the work and acquired great familiarity with engines. At about the latter end of World War 1 Herbert married Ethel Driver. They had no children.

He bought vehicles of his own when the war was over. He once brought over to Mirfield a motorcycle and side-car which he hoped to persuade my father to buy so that I could travel to Leeds University with it. He took me for a trial run in it. Of course, there was no deal.

Later Herbert had a three-wheeler Morgan. On these vehicles almost the whole of the engine was visible from the front. The rear wheel danced when cornering. Herbert moved over to the little four-wheel Jowett tourer, made in Bradford. He could take the engine to pieces and reassemble it, once chopping off the tip of a finger in tilting the engine back into place after

Joseph H Hird

de-carbonising.

He and Ethel became fond of camping, competitions in treasure-hunting and map-reading with the Bradford Gypsy Club. Herbert won a cup for this. The Jowett was so manageable that once on a competition run when there was a puncture some farm workers watching lifted the car up while Herbert changed the wheel and he was soon off.

In 1922 on the occasion of my marriage Herbert gave me the surprise of being present at Holy Trinity Church, along with Edward. They were the only people connected with me.

In 1926 I started motoring, with a 2½ horsepower AJS motorbike. After a time with this plus side-car, it was decided to have a car. As I knew Herbert was familiar with motors I consulted him, and through him bought a Jowett 4-seater tourer (with hood roof). By coincidence Annie now deals with the same garage, Jagger's of Horton Bank Top, forty years later.

There was no driving test at that time and I drove on an outing next day and used the car for school on the following Monday. I parked the car in the Technical College yard opposite the school. Going to it after school I had to reverse in order to turn and come out of the yard. Having started the rearward movement I suddenly realised that we had not given much thought to this way of proceeding. Pressing the wrong pedal, I arrived at the wall fifteen yards behind with a resounding bang which knocked in a rear corner of the car, to the great delight of some Form Four boys watching me.

We lived at Shelf then, and Herbert appeared for decarbonising the car, and incidentally discussed gardening with Annie. There was talk about his camping with his car and we followed suit, visiting places he had recommended, notably Filey and Bridlington.

Like Ernest Herbert had an ambition to be a businessman. He could have been a motor driver, but he knew such men would be 'ten a penny' after the war, and he reserved his motoring for his hobby, while continuing to make his living as a packer. His move towards business was by starting a Clothing Club, using his car to go round to houses where women acted as his agents. Keighley was his main centre, and he visited people who had given orders. He did the measuring for the garments. He measured my son Brian for an overcoat, but it was not satisfactory. When my mother came to live near us, Herbert approached her for a loan of money to develop his business, but failed. My mother said he "soopped al t' profit".

Some years later he began to suffer with stomach trouble. After a period in hospital he left his packing work and became a chauffeur for a gentleman. I met him in town standing by the fine car, ready to open the door. He was delighted with the privilege of driving such a vehicle.

This did not last long. Stomach trouble recurred. My Uncle Ernest took Herbert to hospital and he died at Easter 1955, aged 65 while I was away

Joseph H Hird

at Broadstairs on a visit with a group of children from St Martin's School. His widow had to go round trying to disentangle the Clothing Club business. She has remained in the Corporation (Council) house he was able to obtain as an ex-serviceman.

As a self-made man Herbert had been much less successful than Ernest. Both had tried the same method of achieving independence, squeezing in as individuals and with little capital into businesses run on a large scale by companies.

Edward

Uncle Edward was young enough to play with Lewis and me when we occasionally met. Once my Grandmother Brown brought the two lads and spent a night with me at Kitson Hill. Sleeping was difficult. We three boys had the same bed, they in the normal position with me between them and with my head between their feet. Edward was active and proudly showed me the development of his muscles. His biceps stood up like apples. He amused me by calling our road a street. There were no streets near where we lived.

I went to stay at Rydal Street in Bowling at my grandmother's. Edward and some lads were trying to play cricket in the cramped area of the back garden with a hard ball. I happened to go to the door and was hit in the right eye, which has been weaker in vision ever since.

Edward seems to have made no effort to 'improve' himself. At one time as a boy he attended a

Band of Hope, a kind of temperance organisation, but this appeal did not have a lasting benefit for him.

When World War 1 came he joined the Bradford Pals. This battalion and the Leeds Pals suffered terrible losses in the attack on German positions on the Somme on July 1st 1916, but it was Edward's luck to be sent to Salonika in the confused strategy of the attempt to move round the southern side of the German allies and link with Russia. At Salonika there was little else but discomfort and the boredom of planless waiting.

After the war Edward shuffled on. He married and stayed with his mother. There were no children. Edward drank and kept bad company. My Aunt Martha met him in the street in Bradford once, begging, and gave him a good talking-to. He came to see me at Carlton High School once and asked for a loan of ten shillings. I gave him fifteen shillings.

When my Grandmother Brown (still in the house at 24 Frimley Street, Little Horton, unchanged to this day) entered upon her last illness, she owed much to the attention of Ernest's wife, who had come upon the scene in her last years.

Ernest died aged forty-nine. His wife came to our house to tell me about the funeral. She said she knew Edward had been 'a bad un'. I said I would speak to my mother about it. She said it was not suitable to go to Edward's funeral; he had behaved so badly. I think I was mistaken in not trying harder to persuade my mother to overlook Edward's past, if only for the sake of the woman who had stood by him.

Lewis

The last and eighth son Lewis, nearest to my age, and so a playmate for me on the rare occasions when we met at Mirfield or at Rydal Street, was the 'softest' son. He had a doll, dressed as a sailor, which we buried in the garden when it broke, Lewis conducting the ceremony. Near this grave was a box with wire netting where Lewis fed a rabbit on bran and tea leaves.

Lewis had none of the forceful energy of Edward, but he was ambitious to become a professional man and started on a correspondence course for architecture. On the last occasion when I saw him he was working on large drawings in the little bedroom at 24 Frimley Street. Circumstances prevented any long-term test of his character. He was called up into the Army and killed a few days before the Armistice. He was twenty-four. After the war there were organised visits for relatives to go to war cemeteries to try to find names on the crosses. My Aunt Martha went on one of these, the next of kin, my grandmother, being too old. I did not hear that Martha was successful.

With regard to their position in life my Brown uncles can be seen as falling into two groups, those staying where they happened to find themselves and those wanting to 'better themselves'. Rufus, the eldest, stayed in the dyehouse, near at hand and where he had joined his father. He remained steady, but Tom, James and Edward shifted, getting no higher, Tom and Edward at times passing beyond the borderline of respectability. Arthur, Ernest and Herbert felt an urge; Arthur and Ernest succeeded.

2

My Hird Uncles and Aunts

My grandparents on my father's side were dead long before I was born. They had been born towards the end of the first half of the nineteenth century, and my Grandfather Hird died so young that my father could remember hardly anything of him. My Grandmother Hird (née Horrocks) died six years before I was born. But I did get to know my Hird uncles and aunts.

Joe

Though my second name, Henry, came from a brother of my father's mother, Henry Horrocks, my first name, Joseph, was given me after my father's brother Joe.

None of the three sons of my grandfather, John Hird, followed him into the forge at Low Moor, where he had been a puddler. The family had moved down to Low Moor from Clayton Heights, then a more rural place. In Low Moor there was more variety of work available. The Industrial Revolution had led to a great development of the textile mills in the Bradford area, an advantage being that coal was mined locally. There was weaving at Low Moor as well as at other places within walking distance, such as Wibsey and Oakenshaw, as well as down Manchester Road towards Bradford.

My Uncle Joe was a greaser at a mill in Thornton Road, beyond the centre of Bradford. Such more distant work was possible after the introduction of trams.

He was easy-going and unambitious. He liked the social side of his work so much that he used to arrive at the mill half-an-hour before starting time in the morning, even though that was early (mills used to start at six). The men used to discuss sport mainly, getting their information from "t'issher", the sports edition (issue) of the evening newspaper. Joe liked the warm engine-room. So far as the sport was concerned, Joe's interest must have been based on hearsay. I never heard of his attending a match.

Uncle Joe did not stir far from the place where he was born, at Portland Street. He lived at 27 Draughton Street, Bankfoot, very convenient for his tram to Bradford and for Low Moor, where he went to see his brother Ben and sometimes his three sisters. The ownership of the house where the family had lived had fallen to Joe as the eldest son. My father had the idea that eventually this property should come to me as I should be the only descendant to carry on the name. In the event, however, it went to Joe's widow and then to a nephew of hers, Mr Pearson.

I went to see my Uncle Joe when I was on leave from my war service in the navy. He took me across the street to visit some people called Riley. Mrs Riley had been a weaving neighbour of my mother's before we went to Mirfield, and there had been one or two Sunday visits to Mirfield from Low Moor in our early years there. These were the only occasions when I remember seeing bought beer on our table. On this visit Joe told me a discouraging story of another lad in the navy, also a neighbour, who had spent hours in the sea when the cruisers "Cressy", 'Hogue" and "Aboukir" were torpedoed.

After he retired, Joe came a few times to see us at Shelf, a convenient journey as the tram terminus was near our house at Bridle Stile Lane. He was jolly and blustering. He was too fat, eating too much as well as drinking, being a habitué at The Woodman Inn at Bankfoot. Having no other hobby but talking, he found the public house the most convenient place for indulging in conversation.

On one occasion he wanted Annie and me to try to tune a curious upright piano acquired long before at a sale at Low Moor Vicarage. We found the wires breaking under our attempt to tune them and we stopped before rendering the instrument soundless. That piano was an example of the harbouring for the sake of 'respectability' articles of furniture which were useless and an obstruction.

Joe admired the music we made at Shelf but without discrimination. He also admired a neighbour living at the back of the house in Draughton Street, and we had to go to hear how this man could play the piano using the sides of his hands only, like choppers.

Joe had not much taste in music and what he had must have come late. When he was a boy my father acquired a concertina, but "Aar Jooe paused it art o't door." That was my father's only attempt to gain any kind of musical proficiency.

I may add here that my father liked to sing a phrase or two of songs he had heard at the Music Hall. It was always on a Sunday morning when this fad came over him, he having risen and left my mother in bed, the only morning when she could lie in a little.

Joseph H Hird

After he had drawled out several times the same phrase such as *Bonny Mary of Argyle* at intervals during his manoeuvres over kindling the wood fire, she would reach out of bed and send one of her boots hurtling down the steps and against the door at the bottom.

There was no spirit of adventure in Joe. He would not go away for a holiday, a possibility in the latter part of his life; there had never been any thought of going for holidays in the younger days. Joe refused to be away from home at night and sleep in any bed but his own. The time came when he had to go to hospital for an operation. They wanted to give him a bath. He tried to refuse. He had never had a bath. He said: "No. Ah mun keep art o't watter!".

My Uncle Joe did not feel at ease in the use of indoor sanitation. He preferred, when he visited us at Shelf, to go into the garden, although I indicated the way to the bathroom.

My coming to live and work in this district did nothing to bring together the youngest brothers, my father Sam and Joe. They never visited each other. After long years of absence they met at the funeral of their oldest sister, Sarah. They did not speak. Joe thought the younger brother should make the approach. Sam, remembering Joe's former 'bossy' attitude, was too proud to do so.   Sarah (née Pearson) was Joe's second wife. He had been formerly married **to** a woman from Low Moor called Bywater. When she died Joe was on one occasion in Cobbler Pearson's and was advised by this man, one of Joe's cronies, to look out for another wife. Joe said he had thought about this and he knew just the right woman. When Cobbler Pearson asked who it was, Joe said "Your Sarah!". The friendship ended abruptly, but Joe married Sarah.

Joe came to an abrupt end. In 1932 he went with his wife Sarah to the barrier at Bankfoot to wait for a tram for Low Moor, and sank down and died He was about 72.

Sarah, Annie's mother and Aunt Rose knew each other very well, and had done so from childhood. Sarah attended the Mother's Union meetings at Holy Trinity Church quite regularly, when as a widow she came back to Low Moor. She had had very little education. Once when the vicar's wife enquired about her health she said she had had 'Brown Titus' (bronchitis).

Ben

My Uncle Ben remained in the cottage at Portland Street, Low Moor. He never married and continued to live alone, with the house about as bare as a hermit's cell. It had one room, a stone sink, a table, a chair and an alcove for a bed.

At one time he went into partnership with another man in a coal-delivery business. It failed because, my father said, he gave too much over-weight. In later years he, like my Uncle Joe, became a greaser in a mill in Bradford, down Manchester Road just below Roundhill Street. He became involved in gambling as a pastime and on one occasion was swept up in a police raid.

My father had sympathy for Ben. They were the last of the six children and had shuffled along together in the years between my Grandmother Hird's death and my father's departure to Hird Road.

During my childhood we rarely went to Low Moor. When we did, the main aim was for my father to 'look at' Ben. During these calls my mother and I sat in my Aunt Olive's nearby, in North Street. Ben could not endure company. I have heard my father broach the idea of his coming to live with us at

Mirfield. My mother listened and said nothing. It would have been impossible; we had no room and the kind of life we were living, psychologically, would have made the scheme outrageous. In his last years my cousins, Olive's daughters, used to take Ben his Sunday dinner, but he did not go to see any of them or want anyone to intrude on him.

When Annie and I lived with Aunt Rose nearby, I tried to visit and talk to him., but he made little response. It was like trying to awake a prisoner in the Bastille. He would not take up any cue I gave. He replied every time with "Aye, it is, don't yer know."; or "No, it isn't, don't yer know." On one occasion I saw him near the bottom of Manchester Road. He was standing in a doorway on the site where the Odeon Cinema is now and looking up at the buildings opposite while he took some sort of food from his pocket and threw it into his mouth. I stood in a doorway opposite wondering whether to approach him, but it seemed impossible to get through to his mind. He was watching an upper floor and, as I knew that it was in Manchester Road that the raid on gamblers had taken place, it may have been that he was watching to go in to one of their sessions.

When my father died my mother wanted Ben to be present at the funeral. My cousins tried to smarten him up but he was ill at ease. He moved through the proceedings of the meeting at our house at Kitson Hill Road like a mute, while Aunt Olive's daughters did the talking. After the funeral at Mirfield Parish Church, there was a tea at Battyeford Parish Room, the one where in January 1901 I had begun my schooling. He showed how unused he was to eating with other people, taking sandwiches from the plate, breaking off pieces below on his lap and stuffing the food into his mouth.

My mother kept him in mind after my father's death, and though she never went to see him, she took care to have him buried in my Grandmother Hird's grave at Holy Trinity Church.

Sarah

Of my father's three sisters, Sarah was the eldest. She married a man called Walter Groves. There were three children, Minnie (I thus had two cousins called Minnie on my father's side), Florrie (I had two of this name, this time one on my mother's side and one on my father's), and John William. Of these the boy was younger than me. I remember him in a photograph with a sailor suit (I had had such a suit myself in the Infants' School).

The family lived in Roundhill Street down Manchester Road, only a few minutes' walk from our house, but the back-to-back houses have now been replaced by tall flats surrounded by grass.

Walter Groves turned out to be a drinker. Once when my father and I were visiting on a Saturday afternoon, he came in from the pub. He always had a blustering form of hospitality and on this occasion was dissatisfied with what Sarah had cooked in a frying pan and flung it on the fire. Sarah was ashamed of him and soothingly apologetic to us. I have heard my father say: "Walt'd gi' me 'is last ˢawp'ni," but there was no explanation of this long past obligation which was, it seems, the cause of Walter's exigent hospitality.

Once when Walter came home merry he brought some pub cronies with him and ordered his daughter Minnie, who had acquired a little skill with the accordion, to get up out of bed to play for the company.

Joseph H Hird

During the time when Minnie was courting we happened to visit on a Sunday. Her young man took me to Sunday School where he was a teacher. For their wedding (which we did not attend) my father made a set of fire-irons at his forge, ie poker, coal-rake and tongs. Our visit to deliver these was the last occasion on which I saw Minnie. She died early in the marriage in childbirth. The sight of her in the coffin was one of the first occasions when I saw a corpse. We had received a photograph of her in her wedding dress. The two ways in which she was dressed seemed to me curiously similar.

Florrie married somewhere in the neighbourhood, but we lost sight of her and of John Willie. As a boy he liked playing football in the street. We were once there when he hurried in, took very little notice of us, devoured a teacake and rushed out again.

Sarah died while I was away at the war. She had been a wearily toiling woman but buoyant.

Many years later Walter was navvying with a gang of Corporation men in the street outside Carlton School. He somehow knew I was there and asked his foreman if he could stop work early so that I could take him home in the Jowett car in which at that time I travelled. In view of his rough way of living it was remarkable that he could do such physical work at that age.

Mary Ann

My Aunt Mary Ann married a man called Wilkinson Farrer. They lived at Portland Street, Hill Top, in the original house, in the part adjoining my Uncle Joe's solitary part. There were no children. She died young of cancer.

Olive

A unt Olive also settled a few yards away from where she had been born. She married Sugden Dalby, a stout, cheerful clubman. He was an engine driver at the Low Moor Works, where the company had its own railway. This linked with the Lancashire and Yorkshire Railway as well as with its own 'waggon road' running from Low Moor across country to the series of pits extending to my father's pit at The Three Nuns, Mirfield, many miles away.

One Sunday I went on the engine with Sugden. I was nervous about the passage over the tall, slender bridge with no sort of support or protection. I could see nothing but space beyond the narrow footplate. In the shed I found it fascinating to watch the opening of the blast furnace and the running of the iron in channels in the sand to form pig-iron. The cooking of the coal being turned into coke was impressive also.

Olive and Sugden had six daughters. I believe all are still living except Ida. *In the photograph they are (left*

Joseph H Hird

*to right back row) Martha Harriet, Ida, Elsie; (front row) Maud, Alice, Minnie).*The girls all went into weaving, available a few yards from the door, and for recreation went to the 'Tin Chapel' also only a few yards away. The great occasions there were the anniversaries when the children 'sat up' in the field outside the chapel and there was fiery preaching and fervent singing, with the wooden collection box of characteristic shape coming round clattering the coins during the last hymn. It was said that boxes were preferred to bags for these large open-air gatherings, because they admitted the tips of the fingers only and the drop of the coin could be heard, whereas with the bags it was not possible to be sure whether something was being put in or taken out.

Sunday was a day for hearty eating, and there was no disapproval of Sugden's expenditure of time and money at the Club. Once, however, when I was there he mentioned that he wanted a button sewing on; he was censured for suggesting such a thing on a Sunday.

Olive survived Sugden, finishing her days sedentary and with joints swollen. She died before him in the year of my father's death, 1937.

All the six daughters of Olive married, but from them came only two sons. Maud married Herbert Racher and had a son Charles and two daughters. My father had been displeased with my departure from home with my approaching marriage and this tension became known to Herbert. He had got work which saved him from having to do military service, and when the war was over became a teamer at a flourmill at Wyke. He paid visits to Mirfield, particularly when broadcasting started, helping my father in the fitting of a wireless set. In the late twenties, however, these visits ceased.

Ida married a man called Laycock and ran a fish and chip business, first in a wooden hut at Hill

Yorkshire Folk in the Early 1900s

Top, then in a shop at the corner of School Street. They had a son, Kenneth. He went to Grange High School, so I missed seeing him at Carlton School (but Charlie Racher came to Carlton, to be the third relation I met there, as long afterwards the grandson of Rufus and son of my cousin Arthur Edward Brown, another Kenneth, came there). Ida died at the age of forty-six in mental disturbance, said to be consequential on the change of life.

Later Elsie, the youngest, also went to Menston Hospital, where I believe she still is, though I do not know what was the cause of her affliction. She had married a Co-op man called Widdop.

Alice's husband was called Cordingley. They went to live at Bailiff Bridge about three miles away, too far from her sisters, even though she was only a few yards from the tram terminus. Mr Cordingley had a double means of income, as bookmaker's clerk and barman at a public house.

Martha Harriet married a Barraclough and Minnie a Furniss, both husbands being textile workers. Martha and Minnie and the other surviving sisters live close to the spot where they were born, their greatest pleasure being each other's company. Alice's husband had the courage to say that his wife's sisters spent too such time in each other's houses. This detached view made him unpopular.

Among my relations of the previous generation the men tended to spend their leisure in the pub or working men's club, the women not going out of the house in leisure time except to gossip with each other. The men who married my Aunt Olive's daughters were, with one exception, all sit-at-homes, with Sunday chapel.

In the generation after mine there was more interest in games. Charlie Racher liked winning. Bradford schools were uniquely forward in providing swimming instruction. Charlie's swimming came in useful later when he got a Royal Humane Society's award for rescuing someone from the sea at Blackpool. He also learned to play the piano and was organist at the new chapel which took the place of the Tin Chapel. Later he entered upon a marriage which foundered.

Although my cousins live so near, I have seldom met any of them. Martha Harriet at one time lived a few doors from us when we were with Aunt Rose at 44 Manor Row, Hill Top, Low Moor, and we could frequently have a passing word, especially on a Friday evening when she happened to be washing the flags outside the back door. This was an operation carried out on the knees. My mother spent much time in this position on our flags every Friday night at Mirfield.

The abandonment of a routine of day work and physical activity in housework has often been a factor in obesity. I saw Martha Harriet recently with her husband in the Fish Market and was astonished at her size. Her diameter must have been quite half her height. Eating as a pastime has become prevalent.

The other sisters, however, have not gone that way. I met Minnie on the bus some years ago as I was returning from school at Brighouse. She was wanting a song to sing at a Women's Bright Hour. I went with her. She bought *When I grow too old to dream*.

Recently I attended Herbert Racher's funeral at the Chapel at Low Moor. I had no conversation with my cousins. Alice, long a widow, seemed well preserved, but Maud, the bereaved, was almost bent double and needing support.

The gentleman, presumably a visiting lay preacher, who officiated at the funeral had, it seems, had time to pick up only one fact about Herbert: he had been in the choir a long time. This demonstration of leadership in praise of The Lord formed the middle part of the address, the opening having been a multitudinous paraphrasing of the idea that it is a pity when anyone dies. In the conclusion the speaker dropped unusually into a minor key. Herbert had been a sinner, but God knew that and would purge him, and we must have the Christian hope that God would forgive him and receive him.

That address at the last funeral I have attended up to the present showed the awkward position a visiting minister is put into when he feels it incumbent upon him to make reference to a particular person about whom he knows little.

When I entered the house for my Uncle Ernest's funeral, I was astonished at the cheerful tone punctuated with laughter in the conversation between the widow and daughter and their friends who had come into his life only near the end. The entry of the minister was an abrupt reminder of the object of the gathering. At the church the address was of a pattern suitable for any funeral except for the one detail of personal reference, that Mr Brown had lived a fair long time but it would have been good if he had lived a little longer. This the minister said with a pleasant grin at the widow and step-daughter.

3

The Harkers and Bottomleys

Annie's family first set up house at Angel Court, near The British Queen in Huddersfield Road. (Only the name now remains, the houses having been demolished.) They then moved to 46 Manor Row, Low Moor. This house was at right angles to number 44, where, after we married, Annie and I were to live with Annie's Aunt Rose Harker, who was still in the house where she had been born sixty years earlier. This house had been built by Annie's great- grandfather John Harker, a joiner. He was born in 1801. He married Tabitha Wilkinson and three houses were added with a view to leaving one to each child. One of them, Annie's grandfather, William Harker, had been taken there at the age of five in 1843. He lived there until his death in 1919. Annie was born at number 46 on January 8th 1897and remained there until she was 10.

Richard

In the house adjacent to number 44 in Annie's and my time with Aunt Rose Harker, there lived Richard Worsnop. Richard was a son of John Harker's daughter Elizabeth (who had married Charlie Worsnop), one of the children for whom the additions to the original cottage had been made. He was a big man and blind. I had long before heard my father tell of his own courage in fighting a big lad who wanted to bully him. I remember he said he went in with hands and clogs and that this lad afterwards "went blind as a stooan (stone)". Richard was the only person at Low Moor we heard of as being blind, and I wondered whether he had been my father's opponent. They had been neighbours at Hill Top. Although my father said he knew Richard, he gave no details.

The other members of the Worsnop family having departed, Richard was alone. Though blind he got married (perhaps before this calamity: Annie's mother said that he went blind through his addiction to reading). His wife's brain yielded under the strain of his tyrannical behaviour, and the sight of her going out too scantily clad gave a pretext for her removal to the lunatic asylum.

Richard looked after himself. We constantly worried about his setting fire to the house. It was untidy, dirty and stinking, but he managed. He had two occupations. One was making brushes at the Bradford Blind Institute, his white working jacket being stained black and strongly smelling of tar. The other was the preparation of washing liquid, which he transported in a handcart. His leisure was spent in a small public house in Hill Street, Hill Top.

There used to be some curiously disjointed interviews at Aunt Rose's when he wanted something to be looked at which had puzzled him. The two cousins living alone adjacently had a kind of rough, off-hand sympathy for each other.

During the time Annie and I lived with Aunt Rose, there occurred at Holy Trinity Church one of those visits by a priest from some remote parish for a week's intensive activity called missions. Annie and I were in the choir then. The preacher worked up a fervour in himself and infected the congregation. The sufficient degree of hysteria having been developed, the missionary called upon members of the congregation to express individually repentance and to call for help. Annie made one of these efforts. The missionary stimulated each one speaking with: "'Let it come: Let it come. Good!'". The congregation was expected to extend the evangelism to non-attenders. Annie thought that Richard Worsnop might be persuaded to go. Her effort had a humorous effect. He was obviously not interested in being evangelised, but he would go if he could be fitted up with clothes to make him look smart enough. The mission was fruitless as far as he was concerned.

To tell the time Richard had a clock with large hands which he could feel. He occasionally came in to ask what time it was when his clock had stopped. Even with his clock, he confused day and night and we could hear him noisily active during the night. He was given to bursting into song. During that time Annie was a contralto soloist and member of William Mallinson's Quartet Party. Her practising made Richard next door envious and gave him the illusion that he also was gifted that way. We could hear his pushing and straining his way up the scale.

Eventually public-house, dirt and inadequate feeding caused Richard to soften his independence and allow visits from Dr Leake. On one of these occasions Richard was found in a hazy condition sitting on the cellar steps. He was moved to the hospital, and it was reported that the shock of being given a bath killed him.

Richard's brother, a Wibsey man, steady, cheerful and chapel-going, called occasionally and sat for a while when he came 'to look at' Richard. Annie helped him to get through the legal business of the succession to the ownership of the house. For this Annie was given a chair, which has ever since been a piece of our household furniture.

William

Annie's mother, Mary Ellen, was a daughter of John Harker's son, William. She was the oldest of his four surviving children, three boys (John, Henry and James) having died in infancy. Mary Ellen and Rose and these boys were the children from his first wife, Betty (née Shaw). Betty's grandmother was a cottage weaver and walked every Saturday evening from Oakenshaw to Birkenshaw with the pieces she had woven in the house during the week.

After Betty died in 1873 William married Dinah Wilson with whom he had two sons, Willie and Frank. All the children were born at 44 Manor Row, from where William Harker did not move from the age of five until his death. The two boys, William and Frank, came much later than Mary Ellen and Rose and were nursed by them. When William was born, Mary Ellen was 16 and Rose 14.

William (senior) completed his working life at Low Moor forge, within easy walking distance. I met him in his last months. He was interested that Annie had brought in the grandson of a former neighbour lad, John Hird, who had also worked at the forge. By this time William Harker was feeble, though still able to go in the afternoon to the Harold Club opposite Wright's repair shop where my father and Annie's father had started their careers as strikers before becoming blacksmiths in their own right. The Harold Club was named after Harold Claythorne Hardy (a founder's name handed down from the start of the Low Moor Company in about 1780). Harold had lost

Joseph H Hird

his life in the South African War. Harold Park at Low Moor was also named after him, and contains a gun made at Low Moor and used in the Crimean War.

Annie had given her Grandfather Harker great pleasure on her visits to him by singing at the old piano. There was one song in which he would try to join in, about *A Hundred Years Ago*. Annie had been frequently in and out as a child before the departure to Mirfield when she was ten. As a little girl she once said she was going to stay and have her tea there. To tease her, her grandfather said that she couldn't stay and have her tea in that house. Annie answered that that was all right; she could have it on the doorstep. This story became one of Aunt Rose's treasures.

William died in 1919 aged eighty-one. He ended his days sitting in his old-style wooden chair at the fireside, with my Aunt Rose kindling in the fire the piece of twisted paper for him to light his clay pipe as his sight became too dim.

Mary Ellen

Mary Ellen was born in 1861 and Rose two years later. They had a busy but narrow routine: mill, domestic work and church, with an annual day-trip to the sea-side. The first time they went to Blackpool was in a railway carriage without top, and the passengers could stride over from one seat to the other. The journey took seven or eight hours. Later they made rare visits to a cousin's at Sheffield. At Christmas time they and their cousins went out with

the wassail-bob (which they pronounced 'weasel-bob') into neighbours' houses and sang *Here we come a-wassailing*. They brewed their own beer at home until someone calling said the place smelled like a public house and offence was taken at this.

The textile mill for the girls was at Hill Top, even nearer than the forge was for their father. It was possible to set the bowl with the flour and yeast to warm in front of the fire and break off at the loom to come up and make the dough. There was, of course, no bought bread.

There were few people at Hill Top who did not know each other. Lads at Low Moor and Wibsey were designated without surname eg "Dooad o' Red Abe's". In the absence of external and non-practical interests, gossip was the principal leisure activity, and it did not interfere with the use of the hands.

Mary Ellen later told me that they felt they had reached a state of affluence when they changed from the candle to the oil lamp to stand on the table.

When Mary Ellen's stepmother, Dinah, was an invalid, there came to Low Moor a kind of clairvoyant who declared that he could cure people without seeing them. Some article of their clothing had to be taken to the meeting and he would describe the person with the complaint. Mary Ellen was sent with such an article and the spiritualist began his description, but was so far wrong that she exclaimed that her stepmother was "Nowt o't sooart!". However she was given something in a medicine bottle, which she told her stepmother to throw away when she returned home.

Rose

Aunt Rose spent by far the greater part of her life in the house at 44 Manor Row. She was born there in 1863 and died there in 1948, but with two periods away when she was in service.

One of these periods was at Newlay near Leeds, where an uncle, Henry Harker, lived in a large, detached house. He was engaged at Leeds Forge, an industry dating back to medieval monks. He was also a shareholder, and when he died there was guessing during the widowhood of Mrs Harker (née Caroline Firth) as to whether the money would go Harker-wise or towards the widow's side, for which prospect visits maintained hope alive. Annie and I accompanied Aunt Rose and Mary Ellen on a visit once to the Newlay house. The old lady was polite, dignified and authoritative. She gave Annie a book of old tunes.

Rose had another period of service with a Miss Potter, reputed to be well-off, who had lived in Low Moor, but later at Shelf. We visited her with Rose. She was fat, gentle, and ready with a broad laugh.

Her father, William, wanted Rose at home and she remained faithfully attentive to him, but not without giving him a tremor of anxiety. She related to us in her later years how she had had an admirer who once got a scolding and a threat for hiding behind a wall in order to intercept and speak with her.

More serious, however, was a visit which came later when her father was retired and felt entirely dependent on her. During the time that Annie's family was at Mirfield (Stocks Bank), there lived next-door-but-one a man called Holdsworth who took to drink. Mary Ellen, who had married Brook Bottomley, both of them being Good Templars, took an interest in this man, who had lost his wife, and helped in his return to steadiness, encouraging him to attend Christ Church, Battyeford The sight of him there, always in the same pew near the front, became familiar to me in the choir. After their return to Low Moor, Annie's parents once brought Mr. Holdsworth over for the day and took him up to Wibsey to see the family of Israel Bottomley, calling at Manor Row on the way. Aunt Rose was surprised when the party left at getting a talking-to from her father, who suspected a scheme by the widower to marry Rose. She ridiculed this fear.

A further attempt was made to win her hand, after her father died in 1919, and it was a testimony to her domestic virtues. There was another widower by the name of Colbert living a few yards away who made himself very agreeable. He called when he could think of a reason for doing so, sometimes having the luck to come when Rose was alone at home. This continued in the period when Annie and I were living there. But he committed an error of tact. He let it be known that all he would have to do when he decided the right time had come was to hang up his cap at "t'back o't door", and settle in. There was a hook behind Aunties Rose's door, but Mr Colbert's cap never occupied it.

Rose was old-fashioned. She said there used to be a boggard (ghost) prowling at Hill Top, Low Moor. She believed that the way to cure a wart was to prick it with a needle and bury the needle in the garden. To make a fire draw, one should prop the poker up against the ribs. Any sores should be treated with mutton fat.

This reminds me of other homely remedies I had experienced in childhood. When I was at the Copleys I had for a cough a sheet of brown paper thickly plastered with fat stuck on to my chest. For a sore throat my father wound round my neck a long length of 'tar band', thick, oily, yellowish-brown string brought from the pit.

As with Annie's Bottomley family, attendance at church was considered by the Harkers to be meritorious. It was particularly so for Rose. She was

Joseph H Hird

timid about going out of the house, the weather being always liable to treachery. Every exit was preceded by a weather forecast, with much wrapping up if the sky was clouded. Going out was limited to shopping and occasionally, for health's sake, a ten minute walk 'raand t' haases'. When it was raining at church-time, however, Rose dressed up and wrapped up with obvious pleasure in the sacrifice she was making for the sake of doing her duty.

Domestic work had as main tasks cooking, baking and washing. This last operation was done in the small triangular annex added some time after the house was built. It contained a tub for the clothes which were stirred with a 'peggy', and a heavy mangle with thick, wooden rollers. There was a stone sink with a cold-water tap. A water supply and gas were an addition to the original amenities, water having been drawn originally from a well on the hillside behind the house. This well was still usable when we lived with Aunt Rose.

Before the private, domestic mangle came into use, there was communal mangling, run as a business. Some woman might invest in a mangle occupying about half the size of a living room. Annie's mother, Mary Ellen, remembered going to the mangle-house of a widow nearby. Very heavy rollers worked by gears turned from a large wheel at the side could take any size of washed article.

It was a slow, hard operation, but the customers did not regard their attendance as boring. There was seating accommodation for the women waiting, and the meeting under cover, on neutral ground and ostensibly for something necessary, afforded perfect conditions for the main interest: the dissemination of gossip. From this source originated the derogatory comment 'a mangle-house tale', a story having a basis in fact, but exaggerated and embroidered.

Yorkshire Folk in the Early 1900s

Baking and cooking were matters of pride. This pride was taken for granted by the women of that generation. The preparation of dough and the heating in the oven were precisely controlled. There was skill in this when one considers the difficulty of getting the correct amount of heat with a coal fire, supplemented at times with any odd pieces of wood.

Rose could bake a good cake. Like my mother she knew how to get just the right consistency in a sponge loaf. On one occasion, during the year when I lodged with her as a student, I returned at tea-time and she had arranged to be out. When she came back she asked if I had managed. I said I had and she wanted to know what I had had to eat. I said there was a sponge loaf. And what else had I had? I said I had managed with that. The fact was that I was engrossed in something I was reading and had indulged in the incidental pleasure of the sponge loaf till there was none left. This became another family story.

Frank

Frank had a soft spot in Rose's heart. She and Mary Ellen had nursed him as a child, and Frank had stayed at home till about 1912, when he married Cissie, a teacher from Cleckheaton. Rose almost regarded Frank as her lad. He had been in the church choir, played football and had violin lessons. The proudest occasion in music was when he had conducted an orchestra in *Finlandia* at Westfield Chapel School, Wyke.

Frank's working life was spent as a traveller in cloths for a long time for the Bradford firm of A&S Henry, whose fine stone building near the bottom of Leeds Road is now being demolished for town-planning. He then worked for another Bradford firm called Kessler. He called on Rose from time to time at the weekend before going on to Huby, near Harrogate, and Harrogate itself.

This travelling never took Frank beyond England. He said his travelling cost less than 1% of the value of the orders he obtained. He always travelled by rail and taxi, refusing to use a car. At a station he engaged a porter to carry his luggage. His time was spent away from home on working days with a return each weekend. He liked the carefree way of using trains and the leisure to read and believed in the advantages of tobacco and alcoholic beverages for business intercourse.

While living in Bradford, near Bowling Park, in the earlier years after his marriage, he found time to play his violin in a saloon on Manningham Lane. Annie and I visited him, hearing his pianola, and his rendering of Monti's Czardas for me. His playing in a dance band was frowned on by Annie and her mother.

Annie, however, had shared the family admiration for Frank as a violinist in her childhood. In about 1912 she had been a bridesmaid at his wedding, wearing for this occasion a hat with a brim so wide that she had to tilt her head sideways to enter the carriage for the rail journey from Mirfield to Cleckheaton.

Later Frank, now alone after his wife Cissie and daughters Connie and Eileen had died, went to live with his brother Willie who was in his last years at the boarding-house at 4 Bank Square, Southport. The sociability of hotel life and the use of alcohol had, however, become an inconvenient habit, and Willie sent him out and wanted nothing more to do with him.

Frank's son Geoffrey had survived and went into a wool partnership as a commercial traveller in Leeds.

Yorkshire Folk in the Early 1900s

A few months ago (1967) Annie found a telephone number for a G Harker. This was on the occasion of the death of Willie's widow, Aunt Molly (née Forbes, from Bettishill) aged about 92, at Southampton. Molly had retired there to live with her sister and her niece Dr Mary Forbes Black. Annie rang the number and had a conversation, reminding Geoffrey that she and he were the Harker survivors. Annie had been wondering whether Frank was still alive, but learnt that he had died at Southport.

Willie

Willie had left brass-finishing at a firm near the bottom of Manchester Road to be a full-time organist and piano-tuner in Lanarkshire and Port Glasgow He would also come and stay with Rose for a few days. Later visits to Low Moor were regular after Willie and his Scottish wife Molly (Mary) took the boarding-house at Southport. There Willie could play the organ at the weekend at a Methodist Chapel and finally at the Christian Science Church. He would also tune pianos for a Blackburn agency during the week.

Adjustment of religious adherence kept in step with his musical duties. During the period when he was playing at the Christian Science Church, we did not expect an evening spent with us to pass without the conversation turning into a testimony meeting, with Willie repeating evidence that illness was an illusion. The time came when the 'Scientists' wanted a change of organist and Willie could now get through a visit of several days without any testimony. In his decline his willingness to accept medical attention suggested that he had revised his ideas as to the nature of the illusion.

Joseph H Hird

Before going to Scotland (where he qualified as ARCO) Willie had been organist at Holy Trinity, Low Moor, and had kept up acquaintanceships in Low Moor, particularly with a woman, Lily Crowther, with whom he would play duets. He had enough work for a few days of tuning pianos around Low Moor, and enjoyed the cinema and eating out, returning late at night, expecting Rose to provide a huge supper. She liked these visits and the friendly ease recalling the period long ago when the lads were at home.

Willie and Frank had played piano and violin together when they were both at home, taking their coats off for the attack. By the time Willie had finished with that old fretwork-fronted instrument the ivory of the keys in the middle range was almost worn through. Much practising had been done with fingers roughened in brass-finishing. That piano was the first to which I had access in 1921, though I never got far in learning, owing to other activities and lack of energy.

There was a legend that the ancestors of the Harkers were Vikings, to which Annie's blue eyes were tentatively attributed.

Brook Bottomley

Annie's father, Brook Bottomley, was born in 1863 born at Hill Top, Low Moor (as was my father in 1870). Annie, though an only child, was not short of cousins. Brook was one of six children. His brother Harry and his wife Martha had three daughters (Ann, Emily and Elizabeth) and three sons (Walter, John and Frank). His brother Zena had two daughters (Mary and Eliza) and two sons (James and Fred). Another brother Jonas and his wife Ellen Elizabeth (née Gainsborough) had three daughters (Marjorie,

Yorkshire Folk in the Early 1900s

Kathleen and Phyllis) and a son (Charlie). Brook's sister Mary Elizabeth married William Smith and they had three daughters (Minnie, Edith and Laura) and a son (Hector). His brother Samuel and his wife had two sons (Jonas and Eddie) and a daughter (Sarah). (*The photograph is thought to be of Brook in the middle with his mother, brothers and sister.*)

There is no evidence that Brook Bottomley and Sam Hird knew each other well in boyhood, and the difference in age would have rendered any close acquaintance unlikely at that stage. In leisure time they were unlikely to meet. Brook attended the Primitive Methodist Chapel in School Street. At this chapel 'love feasts' were held, where a cup with two handles was passed along and each worshipper received a biscuit; children were admitted. In contrast Sam never became a frequenter of such places, preferring the rough companionship of that youth of about his own age, Herbert Slater.

Forms of employment for both Brook and Sam ran somewhat parallel. Both had experience as mill lads. Brook worked at Buttershaw Mill (on Halifax Road) and my father worked at Wibsey and Cliff Mill, Great Horton. Both moved from mill to positions as strikers at Wright's (pronounced *reets*) repair shop of the Low Moor Coal and Iron Company. This shop at the junction of Abb Scott Lane and Huddersfield Road was the centre for major repairs coming in from the line of coal pits extending in a southerly direction from Low Moor.

Brook moved from Wright's workshop to a similar position on the Lancashire and Yorkshire Railway at Low Moor. Low Moor Station was a junction in both directions. On the one side lines ran to Halifax and to Huddersfield, and on the other to Bradford and Leeds. Brook became a blacksmith and spent part of his time in the repair shop at Low Moor and part of his time on the line with his portable forge, having travelled with it in the guard's van. From time to time he had to spend a working week at some more remote place on the Lancashire and Yorkshire (L&Y) lines.

While he was living at 46 Manor Road, Low Moor before a move to Mirfield, Brook kept a few pigs. There was room for them in the little garden, to be fattened specially for Christmas pork. Brook had firm notions of cleanliness and discipline. He spent time rubbing the pigs down with sawdust and had a method of training them by tapping their noses with the thible while he took his time transferring the food from bucket to trough. He could thus feed them on Sundays when he had put on his best suit for church. When the time came for him to get them out for the journey to the butcher's, it was difficult to persuade the pigs to get off the board as they did not understand this irregularity in the routine.

Brook knew about Mary Ellen Harker and took a fancy to her. She did not fancy him but his mother told him to 'stick'. Eventually his persistence was rewarded, and she accepted him on the grounds that he was a teetotaller and a regular attender at a place of worship, although at that time this was the Primitive Methodist Chapel, whereas the Harkers went to Holy Trinity Church. The absence of mutual affection in the conjugal relationship was never remedied. Before Annie was born, there was a stillborn son.

In 1907 Brook was transferred to Mirfield, also a junction on both sides (Dewsbury, Leeds, and Bradford on the one side and Huddersfield and Halifax on the other). The family found a house at Stocks Bank, Battyeford, Mirfield. Brook died in 1939 at the age of 76.

Annie went to St. Paul's (Church of England) School at Eastthorpe. The Battyeford National School was near their house, but as Annie had been happy at a girls' school at Low Moor (New Works), it was thought more suitable to send her to a girls' school in Mirfield, and she went to St Paul's, though much further away. Thus she and I did not meet in school at the Elementary stage.

Meeting Annie

In the spring of 1909 Annie spoke to me for the first time. We had both sat for the West Riding County Minor Scholarship in March, in the main room of the day school she was then attending. We must have been sitting near each other on that occasion.

My usual occupation on Saturday mornings at that time was distributing newspapers. It came about that when we were waiting for the scholarship results, I was delivering a Temperance paper to the Bottomleys (Annie's parents were Good Templars), and she came to the door and spoke the first words I ever heard her speak. She asked me if I had heard the result. I was surprised to learn that she knew I had tried. I discovered that she was friendly with the daughter of one of our Sunday School superintendents who lived nearby. This girl, Irene Johnson, had been in my class from the time I joined the Infants' School.

In September 1909, Annie and I were put in Form Three (one class) at Mirfield Grammar School. The class was too big, and at the end of the first term a few girls, of whom Annie was one, were moved to the second-year class, Form Four. Annie is a year older than me. We saw less of each other after that, but I do not remember any conversation with her even in the first term until after an event which was the first link across between our two families.

The West Riding County Council had decided to make the scholarship system more widely known. A gathering of the 1909 winners was arranged to take place in Leeds Town Hall. Certificates would be given out and the best one from each school went up to receive his or hers personally from the Bishop of Wakefield. My father had to break time for half a day for this meeting and we went by train, as also did Annie and her mother. It was somewhere during this visit that Mary Ellen Bottomley, seeing my father with me, said to Annie "I know that man". This remark was followed up by Annie when we met again at school, we being in that first term still in the same class.

In 1912 we were again in the same class, Form Six, this being the only class for those who stayed beyond the third year. The County Minor

Yorkshire Folk in the Early 1900s

Scholarship was for three years but could be extended if progress was good enough. In Form Six Annie and I got to know each other better. We were in plays together, and it was known that we were both to go in for teaching. We saw each other in church every Sunday, she in the pew and I in the choir. She helped in the augmented choir when we gave an oratorio on Good Friday. It included *The Crucifixion, Olivet to Calvary* and *Gethsemane to Golgotha*.

At that time one way of obtaining a qualification for entering the teaching profession was by passing the Oxford Senior Examination. Annie and other girls were going to take this in 1913. (*The photograph shows her at age 15.*)

As it was considered necessary to give them extra tuition they stayed in school at the end of the afternoon sometimes. In Form Six we were a small class of about equal numbers of boys and girls, and we enjoyed conversation before and after lessons, sometimes having to be sent out at playtime. It was an extension of this interest that led some boys to wait at the girls' gate to accompany some of our girl classmates part-way home. On one occasion Annie had been detained after school and I waited at the gate. The extra lesson was quite long and it was dark when it ended, and I had not gone home. Annie was surprised and pleased when she came out, and said "I'm going to kiss you for that."

4

My Contact with Village Gentry

In those days there was no supervision of children entering or leaving school, and there were no mothers escorting. It was the custom for a new infant to be taken for initiation by some other infant already established. This system avoided the tearful tension of the first-day infant clinging to its mother.

There was little traffic, the motor vehicle not having yet arrived as a common means of transport. A danger was, however, that there might be a galloping horse, dashing along with a light trap under the lash of a bad-tempered driver. One afternoon at the end of school we rushed up the yard and through the gate as usual, milling about and shouting. I was near the middle of the road when I suddenly felt a sharp blinding pain across my face. A whip had been lashed at me. Its user was Mr Heath who kept a small grocer's ship with beer licence down the road from the school. He was also coachman for the gentleman at Fieldhead, the mansion in the ground opposite the schools and the church, and extending up the hill beyond our house. He was Marmaduke Wormald, of

Joseph H Hird

Wormald and Walker's textile mill at Ravensthorpe.

He used to go to his office by horse-cab and rail. Mr Heath drove his master to Mirfield station or to Cooper Bridge station and met him at one of these on the return at teatime. On the day referred to, the station was Cooper Bridge, and Mr. Heath must have been short of time. I do not know whether the whip gave me a fraction of a second's time to avoid being run over, but the horse was almost on top of me and the driver was high up there, yelling his anger. He galloped on without slackening. Other children went back into school with me, and the teachers, who fortunately had not gone home promptly, applied water to my face. My parents were angry about Mr Heath, and my mother made two visits about my injury, taking me with her to show. She went first to the shop, but got nothing but a quiet stare, and that not from the man himself, and then to the big house to a side door. The complaint did not get past the kitchen.

Marmaduke Wormald belonged to a class far above us working people. He was a familiar sight but only at particular times and in particular places. He would frequently decide that he would walk part way from the station, and then the coachman had to keep pace in the road with his master walking on the causeway in case Mr Wormald should suddenly change his mind and get in.

His wife, Daisy, had been brought up in the parish in a large house called Warren House. Her father, Mr Brook, had somehow lost money and it was Daisy's charm that won the interest of Marmaduke Wormald and saved Warren House and the dignity of Mrs Brook who, now a widow, was able to remain there and keep servants.

Yorkshire Folk in the Early 1900s

When Daisy and Marmaduke married all the pews in the central section of the church were removed for a processional carpet to be laid.

Daisy was pretty and often lively. There used to be a succession of guests at Fieldhead. It was a familiar sight to us up the hill as they would take walks there and along the field paths round the boundary of the estate. The guests were always superior people, speaking high-class English.

With one set of guests, Daisy got the whim to paint a wooden gate leading to the staff and tradesmen's entrance. This afternoon pastime lasted for several days, much to the amusement of us locals. My father enjoyed this episode as he passed the gate every day on his way home. As soon as those guests had gone, a professional painter came and burnt the paint off to make a fresh start.

Sometimes the house party would be on the way back home from the afternoon and pre-dinner stroll when my father was coming up past the church from the pit. He always had some wood with him which he carried supposedly concealed under a flap of his jacket. Daisy noticed this and was heard to refer to my father as "the man with the wood".

Mr Wormald invited men friends in the autumn for a Saturday shooting of crows, which always seemed to nest in a colony. Perhaps there was more *sport* than *need* in the reduction of numbers, for nearly all the fields thereabout were under grass. I watched pigeon-shooting in a cornfield near the Grammar School. In the grass-field there also, gentlemen came for clay pigeon shooting, a somewhat too simple a sport, for the catapult could not send the composition disks very high or very far, and the path of the flight was obvious.

Daisy Wormald had twins twice. As they grew up, the four children had no contact at all with us village children. Up to prep school they were taught at home by a governess, who used to be taken with them for rides in the afternoon in a governess trap.

During my youth at Mirfield the transition from horse-cab to motor-car was beginning. Mr Wormald got a car and a chauffeur. This man lived in the house on the hill just above ours and was conscious of his social position above the manual class. He wore a tight-fitting double-breasted coat, black leggings and a peaked cap. He also kept a well-waxed, long, pointed moustache. If he had any special clothes for attending to the car he was never seen in them away from the garage. Lodging with this man and his wife, at one time, was Mr Wormald's steward. This man was an ex-officer, proud of himself, dignified, non-mixing, and with a well-off accent. He had married one of the servants, a bonny woman. One day, 'passing round the back', I heard her crying broken-hearted oblivious of the open door. The cause of this sensation turned out to be that the 'bachelor' ex-officer was a married man with five children.

In my teens I had a moment's personal contact with the important gentleman, Mr Wormald. In connection with some educational form I had to get the signature of a JP. Mr Wormald was the only magistrate we knew of. A request at the tradesmen's entrance brought the favour of an appointment and I was admitted one evening. My identity was questioned and the signature applied without further interest. My face would have been familiar to him if he had cared to look at the choir during Morning Prayer. (*In the photograph of the choir taken in 1908 Joe, age 10, is to the left behind the curate J E Roberts who is third from the left at the front.*)

Yorkshire Folk in the Early 1900s

At Whitsuntide the procession of Sunday School scholars walking was admitted to the grounds of Fieldhead, where we sang some of the hymns we had been rehearsing every Sunday afternoon during Lent. We youngsters were anxious to get through the round of calls and finish with the solemn things we had been rehearsing. A reward for attendance at Sunday School, as well as the one for a full stamp-book, was the Whitsuntide Tea. There was, by the way, a great improvement in attendance at Sunday School. Returning from our walk we rushed into the school for the 'bun fight'. Several tea urns were waiting and we lined up for pots and a bun, a kind of elongated teacake. There was much jostling and confusion and the floor was soaked with spilt tea. We gobbled up and rushed back to the baskets in the hope of getting an extra bun. When the supply was exhausted more baskets appeared near the door and we passed out, being given an orange as a final gift. Then we ran down to the field where the bandsmen in their smart uniforms came along at six o'clock and formed a square to play, first as a performance and then for dancing. (In my teens I made attempts to join in at this, but the difficulty of circulation in the grass along with my ignorance of what to do with my feet soon brought about a laughing dismissal.)

Joseph H Hird

The hiring of this band, the Duke of Wellington Regimental Band, was a yearly gift from Mr Edward Fairburn, son of a businessman who lived on Kitson Hill in a mansion less grand than Fieldhead. I remember a hot, sunny Whit Monday when Daisy came out to admire the scarlet jackets of the bandsmen. The men were very smart in their red and blue uniforms with their trousers held tight with straps under the insteps. The elderly bandmaster had stripes and several medals. He was one's ideal of a soldier, upright, stern-looking and with waxed and bristling moustache. The whole proceedings stopped after the singing for Daisy to go to him and raise the medals one after the other to hear an account of their origin. She beamed, smiling up at him while we all smiled at her innocence and the soldier's attempt to compromise with his professional air of discipline. Before many years had passed the Company to which that band belonged was at war. Quite early on, one officer was invalided out as a nervous wreck after trench experiences. The church choirs went to Mirfield Parish Church for a memorial service for Captain Wheatley of Hopton Mills.

When Mr Wormald and his wife came occasionally to the Communion at church, it made a difference. During a seven-year period from 1907-1914, we had a curate, J E Roberts, who made a little effort to raise the services out of their long, sleepy dullness. Two candles were lit on the altar for these occasions. After Communion had been made under this new development, as the first altar server I took the large brass plate to the chancel to receive the collection bag. After the service I counted the money in the vestry. Amongst the pennies was a half-crown and there was no doubt about where it had come from.

Yorkshire Folk in the Early 1900s

When the Fieldhead lady and gentleman came to Morning Service, they always arrived late. The curate had already started the Exhortation "Dearly beloved brethren, the Scripture moveth us in sundry places....". When the tread on the tiles of the aisle announced the entry. The curate stopped, turned his head to smile and awaited the settlement of the couple in their chosen empty row before continuing the customary introduction. Departure was similarly distinctive. They went out without taking notice of anyone.

Daisy Wormald's mother, Mrs Walker Brook, continued to live at Warren House, and on Sunday mornings would sometimes walk the short distance to church, always expecting to find that a certain pew in the middle section, near the front was empty. Any inadvertent occupation by a casual visitor had to be corrected by a sidesman. She had no-one in front of her except the little boy probationers, of whom the senior one sat at the end, waiting for a signal from a choir boy appearing at the vestry door to indicate that, owing to an absence, there was an opportunity for one of the probationers to go forward to don cassock and surplice.

I have watched Mrs Walker Brook proceeding up the gangway (aisle). She always wore black of a shiny stiff material, with a long lower garment which trailed behind for about a foot along the floor. It had much pleating and additional material in an involved bunch behind the lower part of the back. For following the service she had her own Prayer Book which she consulted only from time to time. raising for the scrutiny a pair of eyeglasses attached to the end of an ornamental rod, a 'lorgnette'. She did not bring up her visual aid quite as far as her nose, but having assured herself, as it were, that the words were being correctly rendered, she slowly lowered the apparatus and returned her gaze to the stained-glass window at the east end.

When Annie's family began to attend Christ Church after their removal from Low Moor to Mirfield in 1907 her father, Brook, noticed Mrs Walker Brook holding her Prayer Book and not looking at it. He kindly approached her, took the book, found the exact place for her and held it before her, unaware of the dreadful faux pas he was committing.

We choirboys had a respect for Mrs Walker Brook mixed with gratitude. Twice a year we were permitted to go to a side door of Warren House to sing for her. She would appear, listen, smile and say a few kind words. These, at Christmas, were followed by a gift of a pork pie each and, at Easter, with eggs.

Both Fieldhead and Warren House changed their kind of occupation. Mr. Wormald left £147,000, but neither of his sons would retain the house. It became a branch of the Church of England Children's Home, a society which we children at church had known as 'The Waifs and Strays', for which each Lent the curate gave us a stiff little blue collapsible money-box, to be returned on the last Sunday in Lent with as many coppers as we could collect. *(It is now a care home for the elderly.)*

Warren House lowered its dignity by being divided into two dwellings, one half being occupied by a man no higher in status than solicitor and who came to Sunday School to take the 'Top Class' on Sunday mornings alternately, in a separate room. This gentleman, Tom Goodall, long afterwards had the drawing-up and settlement of my father's will.

In due course, progressing in yearly steps up the Sunday School, I arrived at the Top Class. Mr Goodall must have found my way of showing interest satisfactory, for he came some time later to our house to see whether my father would allow me to go to the office as a kind of clerk. We had no idea what this meant, but the discussion was brief as my father had already decided to 'send me in for teaching' and a bursarship, involving a promise to teach, had been accepted from the West Riding County Council..

Mrs Walker Brook had an influence in shaping the course in life of people we knew. The most practically musical people in Mirfield were the Brearley family from Eastthorpe. The father, Gill, was bandmaster of the Mirfield Baptist Military Band. The mother (née Manchester) was a piano teacher. The son, Frank, whom I had first seen playing the drum as a little boy in the band which played at Whitsuntide, his father being a member, became a fine cellist. The daughter, Marion, a little younger than Annie and me, became an excellent pianist, gaining her LRAM and ARCS in her teens. Mrs Walker Brook heard of Marion and asked her to come to Warren House to play. Following on these visits, there was a wish on the part of Marion to migrate from worship at the Baptist Chapel to Christ Church, and it would be helpful if there was some girl who might accompany Marion through the change-over. Marion had not gone to Mirfield Grammar School, to her regret later, but to a little private school in a cottage near their house.

However, Annie was known as a suitable prospective companion, and Marion came. In due course she succeeded to the position of organist. Annie stayed with the Brearleys sometimes, and after the move of Annie's family back to Low Moor, Marion went there for visits.

Marion was somewhat romantic and would take a copy of Tennyson's poems to meditate on during her walks. In our church choir was Irvine Holmes, one of the family occupying the house in the diagonally opposite corner of the block of four where we lived. (His sister Elise had initiated me into the Sunday School at Christ Church on the first Sunday after I was three, the Copleys with whom I had been sent to live a few days before not being given to any form of religious observance of Sunday). In his turn, Irvine became the solo-singer in the choir. He also had the privilege, when the war came and the British Dyeworks at Huddersfield drew off so much water during the service time that the bellows failed, of throwing off his vestments and going into the organ to blow by hand lever. He later got into the Irish Guards and became a smart young fellow.

Marion fell in love with him and they started 'courting'. The association was not welcomed in the Brearley family. There were high aspirations for Marion as a soloist. Such notions were beyond Irvine who, when he left the Elementary school, went into the trade which his brothers followed cobbling.

Time brought a readjustment. When the war was over, there came a new young vicar to Christ Church, Mr Richards, product of the College of the Resurrection next door, and he got as curate another Resurrection man, Harold Pobjoy. He was a tall, handsome figure, returned from the war, during which he had been in Serbia as a chaplain. In education, prestige and social ease there was considerable superiority on the side of Harold. He was interested in drama, and Marion was composer and performer. Joint activity induced a redirection of Marion's affections and a hearty love affair flared up. The abandoned Irvine, recovering, found another less aspiring girl, and let it be known that this time his intention was to marry for beauty.

Yorkshire Folk in the Early 1900s

The Marion-Harold affair reached top priority in parish gossip. The easy, uninhibited demonstrativeness of the couple excited admiration and wonderment: it was so different from the quiet, restrained slow-witted behaviour of the usual courters. One of the best shows was on a certain morning in the week when Marion had to go by train from Cooper Bridge station. The platform was long and high, above the main road from Dewsbury to Huddersfield. During the wait for the train on these mornings much pleasure was given to those whose business took them along that highway, by the sight of the enlaced lovers supporting each other as they strolled backwards and forwards on this open-air stage.

The couple were married in August 1922. They came over to 8 Third. Street, Wesley Place, Low Moor, where Annie lived, to invite her to the ceremony and me to sing in the choir at Christ Church. It was to be the last time I was to sing there, the first being at the beginning of 1907 when I joined as a probationer. The behaviour at Annie's was like that at Mirfield. Harold was jolly. He sang a Somerset folk-song (he was from that area). Marion sat on his knee and squeezed an orange into his mouth.

Mr. Pobjoy became Vicar of Hartshead, a parish adjacent to Christ Church. He and Marion, with the help of her father conducting the Baptist Band, produced the Hartshead Pageant in a field at Hartshead, on part of the farm of Mr Clifford Brook, a former violin player with whom I had been associated in music. The energy and organisation put into these episodes showing local history were remarkable, particularly in view of the sparseness of the population round there.

Joseph H Hird

Annie and I were married on September 2nd 1922 *(see below: Annie's college friend Winifred Bishop was a bridesmaid).*

We went over one Sunday morning to attend service at Hartshead Church and we stayed to lunch with the Pobjoys at the large vicarage. The vicar was full of talk about the Pageant. It had been a great success. Large numbers of 'charas' (charabancs) had come from a wide area in the West Riding, but it had a certain anti-climax. Rain reduced the number of spectators at the last performances so much that a large quantity of food was left over and the hard working players had to organize a committee to go round the parish hawking surplus refreshments.

The decade after the First World War seems to have been a time when optimism and local pride expressed themselves in the historical pageant. Memorable among them was the Bradford Pageant of 1931, held in Peel Park and in every performance of which I took part as a monk and member of the chorus. The scale of this civic effort can be judged by the fact that the producer was paid £500. Our pageant ended just as a great political and economic change came over the country. The notorious 'thirties' had begun.

Mr Pobjoy took a living at East London in South Africa. A difficulty at Hartshead had been that a certain proportion of the salary had to be subtracted for the pension of a previous vicar. Mr Pobjoy became Canon Pobjoy in South Africa. He returned to this country and had further livings in the West Riding. I met him many years later at the opening of an art exhibition at Batley to which Marion's brother Frank Brearley had invited me, but Harold's behaviour was now completely undemonstrative.

Annie and Marion maintained a Christmas card correspondence till last Christmas (1966). We had heard that Frank and Marion and Harold, now retired, had returned to Mirfield. I had written to Frank to say how interesting that was, adding that Mirfield had for me a strength of memories unequalled by those of any other place. He did not reply and there was no Christmas card from Marion. We had obtained the address of the Pobjoys from a man we met on holiday last year at Pitlochry, and who was a sidesman at Mirfield Church which Canon Pobjoy sometimes attended.

Marion wrote in due course a letter of farewell saying that they had built up such a list of names to write to at Christmas, during residence in Harold's seven parishes, that they were going to stop writing entirely. I believe this is the only case where a former friend has written to give politely a hint that there must be no further attempt to maintain communication.

There were acts of kindness from social superiors. Mrs Edmond was one of seven children who lived in the Shelf-Norwood-Green area. Their father was a poacher and had run away from justice. The mother went to the overseer with her children.

Joseph H Hird

He sent her home, saying she had some fine children, and made her an allowance of one shilling and sixpence a week. They rose and went to bed with the sun, stole turnips from the fields, and washed in the beck. For work they got up at four am to walk to Bradford. In her latter days Mrs Edmond spent her Sundays with Annie's parents at Low Moor.

5

Vicars, Curates and Monks

I have counted up to nine places of worship in Mirfield during my time there, evidence not only of the extent of interest but also of the variety. We had Anglican churches (four), Primitive Methodists, Methodists, New Connexion, Moravians and Baptists. I heard of no Roman Catholics: if there had been any they would have had to go to St Paulinus at Dewsbury. Nor did I hear of Jews. The immigrant Jews had gone to live in big towns only.

The Nonconformists' chapels were small, with a simple rectangular shape and an interior very different from that of the Established Church, the emphasis being on preaching and choir singing. Organ, choir and pulpit were all high up at one end, there was no altar, and the pews which filled the whole space were arranged so that everyone on the ground floor and in the gallery could see the preacher. Not having the resources of inherited wealth, the chapels had to rely on the eloquence of the minister for interesting the adherents and encouraging their generosity.

The Primitive Chapel near us was the centre of respectability. Its members believed that they acquired merit by attendance and must be loyal in its support. Putting on best clothes to go to chapel on a Sunday morning was a tacit comment on the behaviour of the non-attenders who made little difference between Sunday and the rest of the week.

Our chapel needed a round of tea-and-concert efforts to raise money, and the great occasion for attracting public interest was the 'sitting up' in summer in an adjacent field. I saw 'sitting up' at the Tin Chapel in Low Moor, but at our chapel in Battyeford it was on a much larger scale. The whole Sunday School was there on the tiers of the stage. A visiting minister gave the address (the Nonconformists did not use the word 'sermon'). The event took place near the public road, which filled with members of the working-class public, an occasion for the girls to show their new frocks. The preacher had to rely on his vocal cords and the fervour which he could put into his examples of sin and redemption. This behaviour gave our Primitives the name of *Ranters*, but on these open air occasions it was successful in attracting a large concourse of working people starved of stimulating interest. Outsiders who had been drawn merely by curiosity risked a sudden confrontation with a collecting-box edging its way through the crowd.

Some Methodist chapels had another open-air occasion, the Whitsuntide Walk, as did our church. These were not money-raising events, but opportunities to bring cheer to infirm elderly members no longer able to maintain their attendance. The walks were entirely a Sunday School affair, with the singing of rehearsed hymns and the leader calling in at the house for a cheery word. The reward was a proper tea for the singers afterwards

As soon as I was three I had been taken simultaneously to day school and to Sunday School at

Yorkshire Folk in the Early 1900s

Battyeford Church, so that I was going to the same set of buildings six days a week, though not actually to the same rooms. At the age of eight two important changes took place. I was re-admitted to full-time residence with my parents and, just before I was nine, I was drafted into the choir via the probationers' pew. Church, from now on, took up much more of my time for many years.

John George Lee was the oldest member our choir at Christ Church and used to arrive at practice late. The nave of the church was in black darkness and we could hear his voice before he came into the light reflected from the chancel. Wherever we happened to be in hymn, psalm or anthem, he would connect with the bass part. His voice was now like a rasp and he had a special way of distorting the vowel sounds. He had been in the choir about fifty years. His late arrival was due to a call intermediate between home and church to get a moistener of beer.

The Vicar, Benjamin Wilson ('Old Benny'), had already been the incumbent for about forty years, but was a healthy gentleman. He had been at Oxford and married a well-to-do lady who did not fail to let it be known where the dominant influence was. She was not in the habit of attending church herself but would come in a horse-cab at the end of service time and scold her Benjamin if he was not ready for the ride home, about three-quarters of a mile. For some unknown reason they did not occupy the vicarage, a pleasant residence in its own grounds adjacent to the church.

There used to be occasionally a celebration of Holy Communion in midweek, with no other congregation than one or two elderly spinsters. One of these was Miss Lister, who lived under our Infants' School. She was supposed to be a kind of 'lady worker', but there seemed to be no work in her position beyond an attempt to get the women together in a Mothers Union. She and Benny, however, found much pleasure in each other's company after the celebration, loitering long between the church and Miss Lister's nearby dwelling in laughing exchange; the tone of intercourse was different from that in the disciplinary supervision of Mrs Wilson.

Benny, old when I joined the choir, now showed little interest in the singing; nor did the curates, never attending any practices and giving no moral support to the keen choirmaster. When there was a sung Communion with parts requiring a vocal lead-in by the celebrant, the few notes of recitative would happen at any vague level, in spite of a cue by the organist. For our take-up he had to butt in with a harsh jerk of the pitch to where it should have been.

The lack of interest in the musical side had not always been so slight. The father of a Grammar School classmate of mine, Arthur Walker, one of the original currier's sons and brother of Godfrey, told me that when he was a choirboy at Christ Church, the vicar gave impositions for absence. A collect had to be learnt and recited to him.

Old Benny did not involve himself much in parish work. It was said that he made no money out of the post. He had formerly patronised a Church Lads' Brigade and had on a wall in the clergy vestry a framed photograph of a large group of boys with the tilted pill-box caps and white sashes. In my time the organisation was weak. I saw boys at drill in the last days of its existence. The exercise was taking place in the girls' yard of our Elementary School. An ex-army sergeant was bawling at the boys just as he must have done on the barrack square with young men who joined because they wanted to be sure of something to eat or because they were misfits. They formed fours and wheeled and marched this way and that. At one time the company may have paraded at church but they did so no more.

This drilling of the Church Lads Brigade was quite in accordance with the association of the Anglican Church with militarism, made evident in the attendance of the Territorials at Christmas. There was verbal militarism in St Paul's advice to don a full suit of armour. In a hymn we exhorted ourselves to beware of the hosts of Midian who were prowling around. We had to 'up and smite them'. We grew accustomed to hearing about massacres in the Old Testament and, from the New Testament, about how the Founder had said he came not to bring peace but a sword. However we heard without heeding; nothing heard or sung seemed to stir any further interest.

Benny kept two curates even in that thinly populated area, one nominally based on Christ Church and the other for a corrugated-iron mission church called St Peter's at the Knowl. He himself had a diminutive mission at The Elbow in the upper room of a house near the Halfpenny Bridge. There were a few chairs and a small cloth-covered altar. There were only two or three boys and the aim seemed to be to uplift ragged urchins in that quarter by reading from the Bible and eyeing a few prayers, marking them present and letting them go, no attempt being made to see closely into their ways of thinking and behaving. By the time I was moving into my teens, he wanted me to take over and asked me to go one evening. It was like a shortened version of our Sunday morning schools, with a passage from the Bible, a lesson from a book and a few prayers, formalities without any attempt to relate to the real lives of the boys. I could only react with dumb bewilderment when the vicar asked me to make myself responsible for the continuation.

Joseph H Hird

In the year following my entry into the choir we got as curate J E Roberts, said to have made a change from teaching. He was with us for seven years. One reason why we had Mr Roberts with us for so long was said to be that he hoped to step into Old Benny's shoes, but the Vicar continued until after the war came, having occupied the position for forty-six years. I knew him only in the last few years when he had lost interest in the incumbency. Perhaps because he had been a teacher, Mr Roberts made some effort to get some content into his sermons, even bordering on the sensational, as when he broached the subject of what are now called 'shot-gun' marriages. Such talk was good for increasing the number of attendances. Mr Roberts left to become Vicar of Longwood, Huddersfield, shortly before war broke out.

There was some difference of quality between the morning and the evening congregations. At Matins the Vicar preached with slow even-toned meandering round his text, to a vacantly staring, day-dreaming congregation. At Evensong the curate preached to some of the same listeners, the twice-every-Sunday faithful, with the addition of some Sunday morning resters and women whose preparation of the joint of beef with Yorkshire pudding precluded any thought of dressing up and going to church before half-past ten.

Quite often Old Benny did not come in the evening and, every year when the Easter activity was over, he went on holiday to Switzerland till Whitsuntide. In summer he found a shorter period of recuperation sufficient, at Harrogate or Ilkley. Neither he nor the curates did any visiting.

Yorkshire Folk in the Early 1900s

In the services there was nothing but repetition from the Prayer Book and the Bible, except for the sermon. Extempore prayer, so important a part of the performance expected of a chapel minister, was unknown. The sermon was always entirely written and read without fervour with head bent down over the desk. During all the many years when I was in the choir, the sermon was an interval for relaxing between standing to sing or kneeling to pray. It was possible to go to sleep aided by the drone of the voice in the pulpit.

One morning that sound stopped, and the vicar did not come down. He had stopped talking because he had lost the place in the sheets of notes. Ironically we were the most interested to listen when he was not saying anything. He grunted and shuffled his papers while we waited for him to round off by reading something which he did not seem to have read already. The notes had got into the wrong order and he had pulled himself up on realising part way down a sheet that he had committed a non sequitur. He could neither give a sermon on the spur of the moment nor go and get one out of the cupboard.

Once there should have been a special preacher, but the preacher had not arrived. Benny packed in extra prayers, but these and extra hymns were insufficient, and the pulpit must be occupied. Benny went up there and did the Commination Service (Ash Wednesday) with us. When at last the vicar retired he left a large quantity of sermon notes in the cupboard in the vestry.

Sermon notes were very important to the curate, too. Like Old Benny, J E Roberts once mislaid his notes. He discovered this after the service had started. His distress was obvious. He stood, thinking, went into the clergy vestry, came out and turned over all the literature in his stall, then, remembering that he

Joseph H Hird

had called in at the Sunday School and might have left his exercise book there, he sent for the key and disappeared. We carried on singing. He came back without the notes and had to go up to the pulpit.. His resort was not to the Commination Service, but to the Bible. He had remembered where his text was to be found and he tried to preach on it without notes. His little, pause-interspersed, circumambulatory paragraphs made his address interesting to listen to, and showed the difference between a sermon from the head and one from paper.

J E Roberts began his Sunday afternoon addresses to us in church with a series of talks on the word 'Watch', taking one letter per Sunday as heading for his discourse. When he was about to leave he asked us whether we could remember how he first began to speak to us. I longed to call out "With the word 'Watch'!", but by that time I was too shy to blurt this out. He got the answer from one of the young women. Some of us who were children in Sunday School classes when the curate began had stayed on to become teachers.

Here I may mention another detail about J E and Sunday afternoons. After our settling into our seats, in church, a noisy, shuffling business, the curate would stand on the chancel steps and say a prayer which we had to repeat after him, phrase by phrase. It included the words "...and profit by what we shall be taught". We thought he said "...and prophecy what we shall be taught". We had done this repetition for a long time when it occurred to him one Sunday to stroll down the aisle on the south side of the nave while we were repeating. I remember this very distinctly as he had arrived just by our pew. (The girls were in the middle pews). I and the other boys of my age repeated "...and prophecy what we shall be taught" quite loudly. We repeated loudly, by the way, because we made the tacit assumption that sincerity and willingness were to be measured by the boldness of our response. On this occasion, J E stopped short and stared at us. We could not understand the glare and the pause. There had not been more noise or clumsy friction amongst us than usual as we lounged with the tips of our fingers and half our faces peeping over the pew-tops. When he had recovered his self-possession, the curate shouted at us " '...and *profit by* what we shall be taught:' Say that". We said it, but it sounded strange to us.

The transformation of the ritual from Low to High came about during the curacy of the J E Roberts. The church grounds and those of the recently settled Community of the Resurrection were contiguous, so that Christ Church was the parish church for the monks, a fact acknowledged in a slight way by the occasional presence at Sunday Evensong of two Fathers in the congregation and the occasional preacher.

When Father Longridge was Superior at the Community, he came several times and I was next to him at the head of my side of the stalls. He was a still, inward man, not having prepared a sermon in advance. After the service got under way, he took out a sheet of notepaper and set down headings and subheadings, and spent the time up to the sermon in contemplation of the paper, now and again adding minor points. His sermons were delivered in a crisp, precise manner, like instructions for a plan of action of which every syllable was important. I have travelled up to Leeds in the same compartment as Father Longridge, when he was on his way to visit the seminary students living in a house in Leeds to attend a degree course at the university. He showed the same concentration as in church, free from all side interests, with attention fixed on his little book and lips moving in distinctly visible but silent articulation. No one in the compartment would have dared to say to him "Good morning. Nice day!"

With close neighbours who were full-time professional ritualists, there seems to have been an uneasy feeling at our church that some change in that direction should be introduced, but what was done was, in my time, slight. Benny the old vicar was dormantly comfortable, and the curate was more interested in expressing himself as a speaker than in ceremony. Moreover, as dissension at other churches showed, when a change from Low to High was rapid, there was wisdom in step by step modification.

When J E Roberts decided to break through the crust of Low Church Christianity, the move made was to introduce a server at Holy Communion. Arthur Neal was the first to take on the new role. He was about ten years older than me, a bachelor with a simple job and no other interest than the church, of which he appointed himself a kind of lay overseer, careful not to be too much involved in doing anything in particular.. But Arthur soon preferred to organise the attendance within the sanctuary rather than appear there often himself, and he induced me to come in. I learned the activities ancillary to the priest's movements and recitations at the altar, and dealt with the collection. before and after the celebration. I was in the clergy vestry, which as a boy I had regarded as a sacred place allowing no admittance to such as us. The handling of the bottle of wine I liked because of the delicious smell. The word Oporto was on the label, and the taste, which I had experienced from the time of my Confirmation at Mirfield Parish Church in March 1910, was the most exquisite I had ever come across.

Yorkshire Folk in the Early 1900s

I joined the Guild of Servants of the Sanctuary and had a medal on a string round my neck. I attended some gatherings of that body. At one of these, at Heckmondwike, I mentioned to a server rather older than me that I should probably become a teacher. He said that was unwise; in his opinion teaching was a mistaken profession. He had tried it and was going in for Holy Orders. He was evidently right from his point of view. Nearly half a century later I read in our Bradford newspaper *Telegraph and Argus* that he was leaving the incumbency of Baildon after a long and successful occupation of that post.

Till there was a change of both vicar and curate at Christ Church, the rise towards ritualism went no further. Old Benny took no initiative in the change from *Low* to *High*, and the introduction of a server at Communion was acquiesced in by him as were the other stunts of the curate. These included the mid-week lectures in the Nab School, lantern services and a waggonette trip. Benny was absent minded and silent about such popularisations, but he had to take a turn in celebrating the eight o'clock Holy Communion. He accepted my activity in the clergy vestry and in the sanctuary, though there I had to move in at the right moments to do the necessary accessory parts that the curate had taught me (with

Joseph H Hird

Arthur Neal's additional coaching), or the vicar would have overlooked my presence. When he was going to stay on to be present at Morning Prayer, he brought his breakfast, including tea in a vacuum flask, an accessory coming down to our level at that time as a wonderful invention. He gave me a little of his un-sweetened tea in the screw-on cap and spoke kindly to me.

When it was clear, a few years later that I should be involved in the war, he gave me ten shillings and a reference. I showed this to the sergeant of marines at the recruiting office in Manchester. He said he would rather have had a testimonial from a po-liceman: "We have no hold on clergymen."

A second curate took the services at St Peter's, Knowl, the little corrugated-iron mission church. These young curates were mostly inexperienced and shy about reading the service and preaching. There was one who read the prayers as deliberately and hesitatingly as if he had never seen them before, and he read his copied sermon in the same manner, with bent head and eyes never lifted from his notes.

The position of curate was occupied by men of a wide difference of character, from the man doing the minimum necessary repetition of routine to the man ambitious to get an incumbency, who would attempt to stir a little life into the sleepy parish. St Peter's had such a man for a time, a Welshman, Mr. Elford, who made a special line of an annual excursion to Holy Island in Northumberland, difficult to organize before the days of motor coaches. He wrote and produced plays on the Northern saints, using the boys in their teens as actors. His sermons also seemed to have their origin in the way he felt.

A curate who came to Christ Church after the war had started was unusual. Mr Whitehead was an MA BSc and had been a schoolmaster in a boarding school. He had intellectual ability and his sermons were like lectures, rewarding careful hearing. He tried to run a special class on Sunday afternoons after church in the choir vestry. It was at one of these that I first heard of mysticism and of the kind of trance possible to the meditative temperament. He invited me to his lodging. He had a fat housekeeper whose son he was patronising, sending him to the Grammar School, and showing patience with the boy's reluctance to be educated. Mr Whitehead talked to me in a relaxed manner about education and interests wider than any I had heard of before. He persuaded me to begin to learn Greek, a knowledge of which he thought basic for a sound education. While talking to me he had within easy reach bottles of beer, and the surface of the table was marred by a large number of rings left by the tumblers from which he was in the habit of sipping while indulging in his literary pleasures.

Mr Whitehead's presence amongst us ceased abruptly. His alcoholic propensity had led to a large debt at the nearby off-licence shop, and his reaction to an ultimatum had been to disappear. The celebrant used to consume all the wine not drunk by the communicants. This duty was not good for the Rev Whitehead with his propensity towards alcoholism.

His sudden departure revealed that, besides his unpaid beer account, he had ordered much more Oporto than had been consumed ritualistically. We heard that he had got a job at the British Dyeworks at Huddersfield, then shooting up into feverish activity following the loss of the source of German dyes. There was a sale of the curate's property in the road at Bracken Hill, one item being several thick volumes of a commentary on the Bible, for which there were no bids till, under the impatience of the auctioneer I bid sixpence. I carried this big pile home. It made me feel that the Bible must be a very difficult book to understand and that preparation for Holy Orders was an exacting task.

After the Rev Whitehead we had a curate who had been a missionary in Chota Nagpur, India, the Rev Finch-Whyte, MA (Dublin). He lodged with his sister up Kitson Hill. He was ill-adjusted to our Yorkshire temperament, and behaved as if he were still among 'natives' of a servant class. He had been used to having a servant always on call, and to having a man to swing a punkah near him to make his night's rest comfortable. At Mirfield he expected to have a big meal provided in the evening and would come home very late and require hot water to be ready in the fireside boiler for a bath. He incurred some indignation among parents by telling the Sunday School children to bring their savings to him and he would send the money to places where it would do a great deal of good.

Mr Finch-Whyte had some interest in learning and had, handy near his easy-chair, a small library of recent books which he had bought. Such voluntary expense merely for the sake of extending one's intellectual interest was something I had not seen before, but his conversation and his sermons did not suggest much depth of thinking. His predecessor, the absconding Rev Whitehead, seemed to me more inclined to conversation having depth and sequence of thought.

On 21st August 1916 we were in the garden at the lodgings of Mr Finch-Whyte when we heard a great 'boom', followed by others. We looked in that direction and saw, rising up above the horizon, a great swirling ball of lurid red and yellow flame. It suddenly changed to black and diffused.

I set off to discover the source. It was the explosion at Low Moor Chemical Works, about seven miles away, and the conflagration we had seen was the content of the gasometer near Low Moor Station. As I approached the scene, there was evidence at New Road Side of the violence of the explosion, in the numerous broken windows and the bustle about a large house at the top of Storr Hill, which had been turned into a temporary headquarters for operations. I met some of my cousins in Hill Top and we spent some hours standing on a pit hill waiting for further happenings. There we were briefly joined by Annie's father, who had been down to their house, not far from the disaster, to see what effect the blast had had. Plaster had fallen from the ceiling and marked the piano. I stayed too long at Low Moor. Transport was disrupted. Herbert Racher, my cousin Maud's husband, lent me his bicycle which I mounted foolishly on steep North Street and from which I fell on turning at the bottom, not having studied the peculiar brakes. I arrived home with a bloody chin and some damage to the acetylene lamp.

The monument in Scholemoor Cemetery, Lidget Green, records the loss of life of several firemen in the disaster. Eighteen were killed or injured.

Till there was a change of both vicar and curate at Christ Church, the rise towards ritualism went no further. Mr. Finch-Whyte tried to introduce confession, but this mystery did not get far. However, I went one evening to it. The curate put on his surplice and went within the rail. I knelt in front of him as if at Communion and said I was given at times to bad thoughts. Questioned as to whether my bad thoughts had been followed by bad deeds with anyone else, I said "No." Absolution was pronounced over me with a gesture of blessing, and I was dismissed with the advice when attacked by bad thoughts to jump on to the vehicle of prayer which, fervently set in motion, would soon carry me beyond the reach of my assailants.

These experiences, together with the Retreat I attended in the year of my confession at the House of the Resurrection, were the high-water mark of my High Churchmanship. The time was approaching for my departure to the war, with the consequent modifications.

Before that, however, it must have been thought that I was a suitable one to be led gently towards a career in Holy Orders. But there was a contrast between what Finch-Whyte said about his vocation and pastoral service to the people, along with the remote sanctimoniousness of his sermons, and his disquieting behaviour in the house towards the good-natured women who had consented to provide food and shelter for him and his sister.

His sister also was an ill-fitting person. She liked to seem busy and pressed for time, setting off suddenly on her bicycle with head high, or deciding to go 'on her pins', and passing people in the road completely ignoring them or challenging with a loud, high-pitched greeting. Between these two and the homely Miss Smith who waited on them, there was constant friction. I was between the two parties, Miss Smith telling me about 'the limit', on the one hand, and the reverend gentleman on the other.

Finch-Whyte showed concern for my spiritual development, and in the vacation gave me some relief from solitude and a change of conversation, from that which I was accustomed to in the evening. One whim of his was to get a motor-cycle and side-car. This was an advance on his bicycle, which to my delight he had invited me to ride a few times, once with a message to the Rev Hone at the vicarage at Upper Hopton, a man who had been a friend of the future Lord Simon, and who later became Bishop of Wakefield. One Wednesday half-holiday afternoon Finch-Whyte asked me to go with him in the sidecar to Dewsbury. Having arrived there, he asked me to keep the motor-cycle's engine warm by stamping on that lever down there, and he hurried off. I stamped many times with no result, and had to stop, leg-weary. Interested men gathered round; tea-time had approached. The mechanism of a motor-cycle engine was a mystery to me, and not much less so to those who were giving me advice about trying this lever and that. There were about half-a-dozen levers, and I told the helpful spectators that I had no other instructions except to kick on the foot lever. I was very anxious about the time, as it was the day for fetching the quart of milk for baking, and I was afraid of my father's anger. When Finch-Whyte at last arrived I regretted having failed to keep the engine warm. He said "Oh! You ought to have done this and this", moving some of the levers. He got the engine running and we moved towards Mirfield. My strict but futile adherence to instructions may have saved me from serious trouble with that dangerous mystery box. I impressed on the curate the seriousness of my being late home. He made the machine rattle and race furiously, and I had a present fear added to my anticipatory one. However, we approached his lodging and I jumped out and ran, to face my father and mother, then getting back on the road towards the farm as quickly as possible.

Finch-Whyte moved away from Mirfield before his role as comic nuisance became too hot for him, but he did not go far. He got a post at a church near Leeds University, and when I went to Leeds he invited me to visit him. I had lunch with him and the man who was curate at St Peter's, Knowl. This man liked Gilbert and Sullivan and merrily sang extracts, one of which was about 'never, never, using a big, big

Joseph H Hird

D'. It was the first time I had heard any of these operas. They did not strike me at that time as being appropriate music and words for a curate.

In spite of my heavy-witted reactions to him, Finch-Whyte did not forget me. He surprised me one afternoon at Knowl Council School, where I was getting my first experience as a temporary assistant. He was at the gate with his motor-cycle and was interested in my progress. I think he was still inclined to push me gently towards the Church.

The successor to Benjamin Wilson as vicar was the Rev Buchanan, who moved into the vicarage. There was no female companion with him. His style showed the change in the direction of High Church. He preached with his eyes closed, lost in rapture, requiring no written notes. His sermons, sung in a high-pitched voice, with head thrown back and half-closed eyes lost in a vague gaze towards the remotest part of the ceiling over the gallery, were fervent with the blessings following, daily devotions and frequent attendance at the .Lord's Table. A bachelor, he invited me to the vicarage where his conversation, or rather his monologue, was like his sermons, not expecting any response, and having no relationship to my experience or anything that might have been in my mind. He was graciously pastoral, was concerned about any spiritual troubles I might be able to bring up for consolation, and whether I felt able yet to enter more definitely on a course of service to the Lord. There was a risk all through the conversation that solicitude might turn to prayer. It did before the interview was up, and he released me after an appeal that grace might guide me. It was holiday time and I went back up the hill to sit alone and let my thoughts return down from the uncomfortable region to which the Rev Buchanan had raised me. He left Mirfield not long afterwards having had, it was said, a nervous breakdown. This was an affliction unknown to us. The general opinion amongst the working people was that strain in a job like that could only be a soft illusion.

Near our cottage in Hird Road was a much larger, detached house where the curate of Holy Trinity Church lodged. He was a Mr Naylor, a nice man whom Annie and I were to meet long afterwards when he was vicar of St Paul's, Buttershaw. Someone came to ask my father to contribute to a fund for sending Mr Naylor on holiday as he needed a change. My father was indignant.

Joseph H Hird

6

The Community of the Resurrection

There appeared for a time in our Sunday School a pleasant, gentlemanly teacher with a style different from that of the inexpert, read-scold-read teachers we usually had. His name was Mr Servante. He had a teaching post at the College of the Resurrection. He invited a few of us to go to the top of the College tower one Sunday after afternoon church to see the pigeons living up there. These birds and their cotes were no novelty but it was a pleasure to meet a teacher so well-disposed to us. In the early days of the College of the Resurrection the

necessary teaching staff could not be entirely composed from the Fathers. Another of the teachers came to help in one of the oratorios that our choir was preparing. He played the piano and was so short-sighted that he held his face near the copy and made it difficult for us ill-controlled choristers to avoid being scolded for rudeness and inattention.

The theological college accepted at that time young men for training, some of whom had not gone far with secondary education, and would prepare them for the Matriculation examination. At the spot where the entrance gates to the College are now, there was an ivy-covered cottage where the first curate I knew at Christ Church had lived. After his promotion to a living, the College used this house for classes, and passers-by could see what was on the blackboard. The room was well lit and the bright light shining out into the gloom of the road attracted attention. I remember seeing a map laid over the board and walked slowly by, sharing for a moment the teacher's instruction.

Geography was one of the subjects chosen for qualification when I sat for Matriculation at Leeds. I happened to be placed for some of the examination papers next to a student whom I had seen on the football field on my Wednesday afternoon holidays. He was a keen, capable player. In the following session I enquired of another of the Mirfield students who had gone up what had become of the lad I had sat next to. The brief answer was: "He's out." I have recently seen a prospectus for the College; the conditions for acceptance are higher than formerly.

The Community of the Resurrection had its origin in Oxford in 1892 when five priests decided to live together under the usual monastic vows, the vow of poverty being modified, however, to permit retention of a member's capital, but only as it stood on entry. Interest and any profits from writing had to

Joseph H Hird

go to the Community. Dr Charles Gore was the founder and first Superior. The five men had as one of their aims to go to some industrial area with a view to contact with the masses. Mirfield was chosen. It was in the West Riding with many large towns in Yorkshire and Lancashire easy of access by rail.

At the bottom of our hill there was a large house on a wooded estate adjacent to two good roads and overlooking the Calder valley deep below. The conditions of seclusion and access to the world were

good. A gentleman called Cook had owned this property. He had been so particular about the views from his house that he had bought a row of houses in the field at the top of the hill, very near where we afterwards went to live, and ordered them to be pulled down. The currier's house and mill by our house had been built out of the stones transferred, the currier, George Walker, being ready at that time to move his machinery out of the outhouse on the yard a little higher up.

The monks came to Mirfield in 1898, the year of my birth and two years before my father was transferred from Low Moor to the Three Nuns Pit then opening. The Fathers, known to us local inhabitants simply as "t' Resurrection men", became a familiar sight from the earliest times I can remember. In their routine they had about two hours in the afternoon for exercise in the open air. This often took

102

the form of a walk out in twos up the hill past our house, round the fields and back via Mirfield Moor. On these walks they made no contacts and did not look about them much. They usually walked in the road, ignoring the causeway.

The sound of a bell in the early morning, at noon and at four pm, reminded 'the world' that the brethren were devotionally thoughtful about the secular life beyond their walls. There was an aid to individual intercession for the world in the form of a crucifix on the inside of the high wall adjacent to the road which skirted the grounds. The sacred image was not visible from the outside. Occasionally we would see a Father calling at Battyeford Post Office nearby or on the way to or from the station, but there was not even a nodding acquaintance with ordinary people.

To the working folk outside the high wall there was something mysterious about the little group of gentlemen who had come to the secluded mansion. They were reverends, as could be seen by their broad brimmed black hats and the collars. They liked buckled shoes, and on short journeys outside the gate they even wore their cassocks with shiny, leather belts.

They had come to settle in a district of Low Church Anglicanism and Nonconformist evangelicalism. We knew of no Roman Catholics in Battyeford, but people who did know about Catholic ways thought that that was what these men really were. Slowly it came to light what their idea was in not going the usual way of clergymen and settling in their vicarages. The Community of the Resurrection was a late outgrowth of the Oxford Movement. Newman and others influenced by him found that the Reformation was wrong and joined Rome. Some, remaining, desired re-animation in the Church of England, and looked for inspiration in the Bible, the Early Fathers' greater diligence in observance of the ritual of the Book of Common Prayer, plus a compromise revival of medieval faith and practice, but with the Reformers' rejection of the Pope as Christ's vicar.

That was, roughly, the view of Dr Charles Gore, the founder. He wanted a monastic routine, with effort outside the numerous daily offices being applied to the study of religious history, writing and preaching. He was a leader in the Anglo-Catholic movement. Some churches 'woke up' and 'went High', with lights, servers, Mass, robes for the celebrant, reference to Our Lady, and everything but the Pope. We heard of dissension in churches in our neighbourhood, where the influence of the Resurrection notions, especially as they came to be gradually worked in by ex-College of the Resurrection students, caused a change in the congregation. Conservatives migrated to impervious, traditional parishes, and young people, liking more colour and gesture, came in.

In the Community itself, this hovering near Rome caused qualms. One of the Fathers was the Rev Benson, son of an Archbishop of Canterbury and brother of A C Benson, author of *From a College Window* and *Land of Hope and Glory*. The requirement of some form of physical work in the younger monk's daily routine had at first a wider scope than the two hour afternoon stroll. Gardening and attention to outdoor work on the estate had a place, and Father Benson's task was to hew stone and arrange the steps for the stairway leading up from the quarry out of which the stone for the Theological College had been taken. He has told how, while his hands laboured, he was also, as Newman had done, brooding over the position of the Church of England. The Solution was unfavourable and he 'went over'.

Yorkshire Folk in the Early 1900s

Charles Gore had, for practical application, the idea that something should be done for the masses. He became a Christian Socialist, writing and speaking about such things as the sweating system and the drink traffic, but these efforts came from the private room or the pulpit or the platform, from the mountain to 'the people' below. The wall round the Community grounds at Mirfield was symbolical. The gentlemen inside ignored the crude, muddled, ignorant and insanitary living surrounding their estate.

I remember Dr Gore coming to preach in our adjacent Christ Church when I was a choirboy. He wore the most gorgeous red robes I had ever seen. He did not stay long in Mirfield. He wrote books and accepted one bishopric after another. The monks had been in our village only four years when the Founder took the Bishopric of Worcester and was henceforth only a visitor.

The successor to Gore as Superior was Father Walter Frere who, like his predecessor, became Bishop of Truro. Frere had a similar idea of service to that of Gore, to write books and preach. He wrote on hymnology amongst other things, and I have heard him preach more often than the founder. He had a charm of delivery and knew nothing about nerves. Once at a quarry service, he sang for a Sunday afternoon audience the chant sung by Augustine and his companions as they opened their mission to England. He would go to watch the college boys at football in their field above our house, and they obviously knew him. On his afternoon walks he talked loudly, gripping firmly a pipe which he held out at half-arm's length and remembered to stick into his mouth from time to time. The two-hour period was for recreation, and he indulged himself deliberately.

Father Frere took part in an act of courage. The presence in our village of these gentlemen who lived in the comfortable seclusion of their estate and did not come out to work or mix with local people, led to an increasing suspicion that there might be some shady behaviour amongst them. It was known that women entered the building, to do women's work such as mending. On the best estimate they were a queer lot. To this was added an attack by the anti-ritualist Kensitites, enthusiastic about the purity of Protestantism. The trend to Anglo-Catholicism found vociferous opposition from the Kensitites, who achieved publicity by a shindy created in London. Father Frere let it be known that on a certain evening, outside the Black Bull in the centre of Mirfield, he would speak and be ready to answer questions. He stood in the yard on a waggon, and began explaining and answering questions. One blunt question, much to the point of the misunderstandings about our strange neighbours, was: "Ah is it yer dooant get wed?". Father Frere's patience and suavity kept the interest and tolerance of his audience till at last the meeting broke up, the speaker up there on the cart and the faces below having become only dimly recognisable in the increasing dusk. The Kensitites did not return to Mirfield, and the locality was confident that those men in the mansion in the grounds might be living a strange sort of life, but they were probably 'all right'.

I came near to Father Frere when the Guild of Servants of the Sanctuary of which I was a member, held a gathering in the Chapel and had tea on the bowling green, The Superior sat amongst us, cheerful and smiling, but it was not easy for us to find anything to say to one so far above us in knowledge and intellect. Knowing that he had a Doctorate of Music for his work on hymnology, the Guild asked if he would give us some coaching in plain-chant. He did not accept but sent one of the Brothers who gave us a lesson in Christ Church. As Bishop of Truro Frere, like Gore, continued to advocate High Church as represented in the new Anglo-Catholic movement independent of Rome.

Among the early members of the Community was Father Paul Bull, a kind of Friar Tuck, round in face and body and inclined to be jolly. He was something of a maverick. He had been a chaplain to the Navy. He declared boldly that the Navy existed to serve God, and it said so in the Articles of War. He had also been a chaplain in the Army in the South African War. On one occasion there he came across a gun stuck in an awkward position and the men cursing it. He suggested another way, a silent one with all possible shoulders, his own included, to the wheels, and the gun moved.

He wrote a good deal but on a much lower plane than that of the Founder. A series of booklets costing one penny was written, called *Mirfield Manuals for the Million*. He wrote some and other Fathers helped. There was one on *A day in a monastery*, explaining how the monks, apparently secluded, were serving the general community by praying for it and preparing for sallying out on missions to parishes. A manual explained the Lord's Prayer; one explained the Creed; a glimpse into Church history was given; 'vocation' was described; Bible reading was encouraged. I obtained several of these in my teens. They tended to induce a vague, sweet feeling of being in a state of grace.

Father Bull was in demand as a speaker: He would make far-fetched jokes 'for the gallery' and introduce striking comment and illustration. Naming a few chemicals, he said his body was made of them and he got a new body every seven years which, he said, pointing to it, was more than could be said of his cassock. At a Sunday afternoon men's service in

Joseph H Hird

Eastbrook Hall in Bradford, he moved us almost to tears by describing his love for his angelic sister who had died shortly before. In the same address he said he was making no attempt to influence his hearers' political views; all the same, he would not conceal the fact that he was a socialist. In his time some platform support was given to the Labour cause, but the Community withdrew from this indiscretion. The address at Eastbrook Hall was given many years ago, and he made a forecast which seems less far-fetched than it did then. He thought 'our future was with China'. Perhaps remembering his practice of mixing with common people when he was in the Forces, he would come into a field on a Saturday afternoon where local lads were at football, and clap and make encouraging remarks

Another Father, Hart, spoke at our Sunday School Prize Distribution, concluding by saying that he must get back, as he had sixty-four children waiting for him. We young ones were puzzled at that. He meant that he was then Warden of the College and must return to his supervisory duties. Later one of the Fathers was to make Mirfield better known than

anyone had previously. Trevor Huddlestone went to work in the South African centre, but found that he could not keep to himself his opinions about social conditions. He wrote a book *Naught for your comfort* and was expelled, but by it his name and that of Mirfield become known nationwide. He moved back to England, became Bishop of Stepney and made broadcasts, attracting large audiences. Then he became Bishop of Mauritius and an Archbishop.

A development of the aims of the Community was the foundation of a Theological College. We could watch the building operations of its chapel in the first decade after we went to Mirfield. On the estate itself was very good red stone, easy to work. The copper domes, now green, are a landmark seen from far along the Calder Valley. The architecture, including the altars, makes the interior very beautiful. A corridor connects the House to the Chapel.

A further development was a retreat house added for the sleeping accommodation of men wishing to spend a weekend or more in a discipline of instruction, prayer, devotional reading and silence.

In 1916 when I had done a year at Leeds University, I went to a retreat in the newly built Retreat House added to the Community building. It was a short retreat of twenty-four hours. The visitors mixed up to supper time. We were given a simple meal (not vegetarian), the silence having started with the sound of the bell for entry to the dining room. A monk read to us an edifying passage while we ate. We went to the

Joseph H Hird

Chapel for prayer and an address, were told the programme for the next day and dismissed to our rooms, with the advice not to pray too much but to give the time mainly to meditation till lights out. The next day we had services and a period of relaxation with a final gathering. The meals again were times for mental sustenance as well as physical. At the end we were released to return 'refreshed and strengthened' to the world.

The other men, I had noticed, came from churches including in particular one in Leeds which had gone 'high' and where the clergy had come under the influence of the Puseyites, Pusey being another leader of the Oxford Movement towards Anglo-Catholicism.

The quarry, left empty after the buildings were finished, was put to use as a place of worship on the afternoons in July. Fathers took turns at preaching, and cards were distributed for hymn singing. I used to hurry along from church in order to get a good place for hearing and seeing. An attempt was made to set together a small orchestra. I joined in at this. These sermons were so popular that, in spite of poor facilities for travel, as many as 5,000 people have been counted by students posted over the exit gate. When it rained it was possible to hold a service in the chapel later, on completion of the Chancel.

At the end of the summer term students prepared a play to be given in the quarry for local inhabitants on the Thursday and for a ticket audience on the Saturday. This was a Founder's Day celebration. Some fine performances were given, enhanced by the natural setting. *Murder in the Cathedral* was one I saw.

In the summer holidays when I was at the Grammar School I would go down to watch the masons shaping the stone for the Chapel. This stone was not obtained from the grounds, and seemed to me inferior. It was soft and red. One day when I was in the house, I saw one of the workmen riding up the hill on the back of another workman, and pretending to steer him by pulling his ears. I thought this an inappropriately funny game to be playing in working hours. But the 'horseman' was only putting a brave face on his pain. He had struck his foot with a pick and was being carried back to his lodgings.

When I was secretary of the football team at the Grammar School I had occasion to call at the College about arranging a match with the secretary of their second team. A word I saw on the notice board while waiting caught my puzzled attention. It was *hebdomadaire*. I found that this heading referred to the weekly roster of duties. Their football was too good for our slight resources. Even with the men on the staff playing with us, we could hardly give the students a reasonable game. We were smaller, did not play frequently enough, and were given no training at all. My position was always at full back. I was not light and quick enough for dribbling.

At one time the field rented for the College football was a few yards above our house, immediately next to the Fieldhead plantation. I used to go and watch on a Saturday afternoon. One day the team had forgotten to bring the lemons to suck at half-time, and the captain asked me to go down to the College to fetch them. He gave me threepence, much above what I usually got for an errand.

On one Saturday afternoon the opposing team was late. After passing some time practising shooting, the students decided to have a sing-song and sat down in two rows facing each other to sing nursery rhymes. I was astonished at these big fellows swaying their shoulders together in rhythm and thoroughly enjoying this childishness.

Joseph H Hird

On their Wednesday afternoon sports relaxation they played rugby, the first time I saw this game. I used to go into the field to the touch line, not realising I was trespassing. At the Saturday games many others did, though some of 'the better sort' out walking looked on from the public road. The Warden, watching one day, suddenly gave us a little shock which we, in our ignorance, thought rather bold. He took off his hat and walked along the touch line taking a collection. It was embarrassing.

At Leeds University I occasionally overheard Resurrection students who were doing their three years there. They preferred the Leeds period and their hostel there to the Mirfield period of two years before and one after Leeds. Mirfield was too 'monastic' for them.

One year there was a student more mature than the average. He was an Australian called Grocer. He was at Mirfield for a year of pastoral training, having already been admitted to orders. His rugby action was a joy to watch. He had great speed, could stride or mince his steps, leap to left or right, feint and elude arms shot out at him, as if he were too greasy to hold. He was not merely a solo player; or rather he was but did not intend to be. When he had not got the ball he would exhort the others, and once he forgot his status and exclaimed: "Run like the Devil!". Other players near him turned to him: "Grocer! And you a clergyman!".

The monks seemed to have had the idea that their vocation had endowed them with some charisma, through which they could convey a blessing. As a Sunday School boy, I was present one Sunday afternoon when Father Figgis came to speak to us, an exceptional situation. Coming from the pulpit he sat on a chair at the top of the steps between the chancel and the nave. We were told to form a queue to go up and kneel, two at a time in front of him so that he could lay his hands on us. Father Neville Figgis was one of the most important writers among the Fathers. He was an authority on *The Divine Right of Kings*. This was my first actual contact, I believe, with a man who had written a book. He received a severe blow when a manuscript of a book was lost in the sinking of his ship in the Atlantic.

In 1910 I went to Mirfield Parish Church with other children for the second Bishop of Wakefield, Dr Eden, to lay his hands on our heads, again two at a time, in the ceremony of confirmation. Many years later I went on a Saturday afternoon to see my parents, and took a walk with my son, Brian. We went into a field to watch a local football match. Father Bull had done the same and stood next to us on the touchline. He was as interesting to watch as the game. At a quiet moment he turned to us, smiled down at Brian and laid his hand on his head by way of blessing. This reminded me that I had once knelt before Father Bull on the chancel steps at Christ Church to receive a prize from him and a laying on of hands at the same time..

The laying on of hands appears to have been thought of as possibly conveying a psychological or physical benefit. It may be that physicists will try to find an explanation, such as the closing of a circuit connecting the strong supply of power from the donor to the recipient. If that is so, I believe that Father Bull, Dr Figgis and Bishop Eden would have accepted the theory, but I cannot be sure that as a result of the two occasions when I received the laying on of hands grace flowed into me. Perhaps the full transmission of power depends not only on its strength in the donor, but also on the sensitivity of the recipient. If that is a condition, how can little children receive the full benefit, being unaware as to what distinguishes a priest's caress from any other?

In the later part of my connection with Mirfield it seemed to me that there was less concentration of literary distinction among the monks. They were no longer individually in permanent residence at the House, Priories having developed in Leeds, London, Wales and elsewhere, most notably in South Africa. There seemed to be some loss of gentlemanly aloofness also. I have seen a Father standing at the side of the main road thumbing a lift, a thing inconceivable of the early Fathers (a supposition, of course, as there was only animal traffic in Mirfield when the first of them came).

I was sitting one winter's night with my mother after my father's death, having gone in the car and left it by the railings, well wrapped up in rugs, when a knock came to the door. It was one of the Fathers, who exclaimed cheerfully: "I wonder if that car is going my way:" It obviously was not, but I went out, unwrapped the car, and took him. He was going to a place a mile away to drop in at a social evening.

Soon after that my mother left Mirfield and I ceased to see anything further of the monks in their habitat. I had first entered their grounds as a very small boy when our Sunday School included the House on our journey round the parish on Whit Monday. While we filled the lawn to sing, the fathers came out and listened and smiled their appreciation.

7

Boarding with the Copleys

Promptly on reaching the age of three in January 1901 I became a Sunday-night-to-Saturday-dinnertime lodger at the Copleys', a few doors away from my home. Thus my mother was now free to resume once more her full-time career as a weaver, interrupted for a month by my birth and resumed when my Aunt Martha looked after me during working hours.

My stay with the Copleys lasted for five years. That family was easy-going. Mr. Copley worked at a currier's shop, smaller than the one near our house. This one was housed in a yard near the Nab School. It later closed down, thus ending the rivalry between the two firms, and leaving the other currier, George Walker and Sons, to thrive and grow into its present extended premises. We did not see much of Mr Copley, as he was away for the six o'clock start before we had come downstairs, and his custom was to return for tea and go out to a club or pub.

Friday evening was rather special as he used to bring home 'savoury ducks' which required cooking and a slower meal. Our usual meals consisted of bread and tea followed by an exit to play out if it was not raining. We did not stay in in the winter but roamed and loitered in the dark or under the faint light of the gas lamps. On a Wednesday there was hash, a gruel made by boiling bones with traces of meat on them, bread being dipped in our dishes. At one time fish, some herring, was offered to me and, being inexperienced, I got a bone stuck in my throat. Not till I was grown up did I ever try herring again. Later I had fish and chips occasionally when I returned to live full-time at home, but that fish was easier to deal with.

I had three occasions of close contact with Mr Copley. He carried me up the hill on his shoulder under a shawl in the dark when I caught measles. One Saturday early in the morning he carried me into the house next door as the Copleys were going out somewhere. Thirdly he attended to me when I ran in screaming because his son Joseph had hit me just on the bone at the side of my right eye when he hurled a piece of broken bowl during a quarrel. It was a lucky escape. I was just turning to see how near Joseph was as he ran after me.

Apart from a feeling of oddity about living near my parents but detached from them, there was some advantage in joining a family. George, older, had a mannish confidence in himself, though he could incur a smacking from his mother as, for example, once when he walked out of the kitchen showing a saucer stuck under a cup by the soap which had got there. George showed it to us amused. The saucer fell off and George got the hand which was ready as soon as his mother saw the demonstration. I also got a smacking, as well as Joseph, one Saturday morning when we had a pillow fight in the bedroom and a pillow went out into Kitson Hill through the open window.

Living in two different houses during the five years from my third birthday, I felt a difference in the behaviour of the two sets of adults who had to do with me. Mr Copley showed a remote indifference. He spoke sharply on occasion, but I had not much fear of physical punishment and I was, in his house, a member of a group of children, so that an outburst of irritation came down with less weight on any individual head. His routine had its advantages for me; he was absent with a long day's work, the evening in the company of other men, and bed.

Mrs Copley, a rather bonny woman with ginger hair, was more volatile. She could shout threats, but she could also burst out laughing. Social interest found sufficient scope in casual visits to and from next door and a little noisy gossip over the garden wall in fine weather. In the house she shuffled through her day. Clearing the table of the pots and things left there after a meal was done to the extent necessary for the next meal. The table was the place where the food was, and it was common to walk about while eating, even in and out of the house. Dawdling untidily dressed was a habit. Mrs Copley's general way of life was that of a happy-go-lucky gypsy.

The return home at the weekend, and the whole week from the time I was eight, had by contrast a certain chill. I was the only child. My father had a more concentrated interest in me than Mr Copley had, but it was apt to be threatening and contemptuous. I lived under a regime of fear. My father spent his leisure almost entirely at home. Club and pub never appealed to him. Between his return from work, often by a quarter to five, and my mother's arrival after six o'clock, there was between my father and me usually a period of tension.

My mother's return was looked forward to. Attention was diverted from me to some extent on to the exchange of news about work and to my father's tirades against his bosses and the characters and behaviour of the workmen. He could be pleasantly interesting when he drifted from criticism to description of activities, events and things at the pit. My mother had her quota of observations about the mill and I liked her talk. It was free from that tone of my father's of blustering, oathful dissatisfaction.

After she had eaten, my mother set about her evening work, which dragged on till a late bedtime, while my father lay back in his chair with feet on the oven, resting his leg with varicose veins, as well as recuperating in general from the day's toil. We were a much enclosed little group with none of that free behaviour and possibility of spontaneous merriment I had shared at the Copleys'.

Mrs Copley had a sister called Ledgard, living just across the river. As bonfire time approached we boys went there to get potatoes, some of which would be roasted at the fire. They did not make good eating as they tended to be partly burnt or raw and mixed with charred wood, but it was fun trying to roast them. At the approach of bonfire night we also did some 'chumping'. We trespassed over the wall on the opposite side of Kitson Hill and into the wood alongside Fieldhead estate to gather fallen wood and wood that we could easily cause to fall. It was exciting mischief for we were at risk of being seen by the farmer, Mr Daniels, while in the wood itself as well as when getting over the wall and to the yard where the bonfire would be. He once did catch some of us opposite our house near the wall by dropping straight down on us, but it was not chumping time and we said we were only looking. For the bonfire we could have old skeps from the currier's mill also.

To get to the Ledgards' we had to cross the Halfpenny Bridge across the river at Battyeford. This toll had to be paid to the man who spent his time almost entirely with nothing to do in a little cabin at the side of the path admitting pedestrians. The rest of the bridge was closed by a gate which the man came out and opened when the occasional horse-drawn vehicle appeared. George Copley said to us once that he would cross without paying. A few yards from the cabin he suddenly put his head down and rushed past the door, the lower part of which was kept closed to make the toll-keeper more comfortable. The man's language showed no consideration for us younger companions.

There were two bedrooms at the Copleys'. The parents had the larger, front room and the three children and myself had the small one over on the hillside. There was a full-sized bed, occupied by Lizzie and the two boys, Lizzie having the side near the wall. For me there was a small cot at the foot.

Lizzie had a sense of dignity and importance. Every night she used to recite a prayer which she rendered like a set speech, expecting quiet attention while she uttered it deliberately. I was impressed with this performance and knew from school and church that it was good to say prayers. I got permission to say the Lord's Prayer and Mrs Copley would stay in the room till I got through it. Lizzie's sense of dignity remained with her and she told Annie later, when the Copleys had gone to live next door to where Annie's family settled, that 'Lizzie' was not a suitable name, and she was going to change it to Phyllis Dedelia.

One morning we were allowed to go into the big bedroom. Mrs Copley lifted the bed clothes part way and showed a little head like a little hairy ball down there. I refused to believe that that baby belonged here, and said it was Hannah Asquith from next door. This fourth child became Nellie Copley.

A relative of Mrs Copley, another Mrs Ledgard, came later to live next door to us up Kitson Hill, and tried to make a little money by selling a few things. A young man, also called Ledgard, looked in there sometimes. I asked my father how he was related to Mrs Ledgard. He said he was a 'chonce un' (chance one, ie illegitimate).

The Copleys removed from Kitson Hill to Stocks Bank Road, about half-a-mile away, but as our leisure time was usually spent in such a small area it seemed as if they were emigrating. The rest of us, from the top of the hill, ie the Holmeses and myself, gathered to watch the cart come out of the gateway and we got up a yell of "Good shutness" as the cart went down the hill with the skid under a wheel and a screech of brakes.

I once in a summer holiday paid a visit to Stocks Bank and stayed for a meal of the old type, tea and bread.

Mrs Copley's reputation for unconcern spread at that house. Annie has told me how Nellie used to appear naked in the doorway and be dressed there, although between Annie's and the Copleys there was a passage, a public way descending from Stocks Bank to the 'Low Road.' Mrs Copley would also go out and leave the door open. A woman neighbour once went to call on her and finding no one in, said: "I'll let that woman know soomdi's been!", and piled all the chairs on to the table.

After the Copley family moved when I was eight, I lived full-time at home, and carried one copy of the house-door key in my jacket pocket. The lock was, of course, of the old-fashioned kind, massive, with a heavy key to fit.

8

Domestic Routine at Home

Except for Saturday mornings, when I rose along with my parents for departure (my father to the Three Nuns Pit, my mother to Learoyd's Trafalgar Mill and I to the newspaper shop and Mirfield Station), the alarm at five o'clock marked the preparation for our separation for the day.

Though my mother's journey on foot to the tram at Bradley passed the end of the cart-road to the pit, my parents never did this walk together. Perhaps a reason for my father's inertia about trying to get a job on the railway was that his day was shorter than was usual for workers. He could leave home after my mother set off on her walk of about two miles. His bosses did not arrive at their office till breakfast time and were satisfied if the work could be seen at a glance to be well begun by then. The day ended between four and five o'clock, when the colliers were all out and the masters gone. My father could then gather a bundle of wood from the joiner's end of the workshop and put it under the flap of his jacket for the walk home.

My Yorkshire Folk in the Early 1900s

My mother returned about an hour and a half later, with one evening a week later still when she called at the Co-op butcher's shop at Bradley to buy some tripe or cow-heel. We gathered round the wet paper and tucked in after dowsing the feast with vinegar and sprinkling with salt. A knife was the only equipment needed.

Normally, then, I was in charge of the house up to my father's return. I was left in bed in the morning and at first an arrangement was made with Mrs Crawshaw, next door, to knock on the wall and wake me so that I could go into their house for tea and teacake before running down the fields to the Nab School. On some mornings I did an errand first, a regular one being to the butcher's shop at the bottom of Bott Hill for shin beef.

Mrs Crawshaw moved slowly and I used to sit on a chair near the door in the quiet, dusty room listening to the kind of bouncing tick of the grandfather clock and watching a little hand jerking round the inset dial, also going a little too far and adjusting itself at each step. Mrs Crawshaw could not move fast. There were swellings on her hands. She was unhappy. We could hear her husband's loud voice at times. He was a blustering man, fireman at the currier's shop a few yards from the door. We boys often went into the shed to look down into the hole where the boiler was, particularly when it was raining, to watch Mr Crawshaw shovelling in coal or pulling clinkers out. He frequently consulted two gauges for steam pressure and height of water. Sometimes he called me to go to the shop to fetch some twist (tobacco). The halfpenny reward was welcome.

Joseph H Hird

Mrs Crawshaw was taken to a lunatic asylum, and there were two consequences. I was now quite on my own, and Mr Crawshaw did a 'moonlight flit' one night.

Between 1906 and 1921 there were three interruptions to my sole charge of the house on working days: a fortnight in 1915, the period of war service and a year in hostel. My meals were simple. For my mid-day meal at school, I took some buttered bread, and usually a piece of cheese or maybe an additional tit-bit such as a couple of biscuits or a bit of custard. During my Elementary School days a pot of tea could be had for one penny at a house nearby and then, in the first years of my attendance at Mirfield Grammar School, at the caretaker's. His wife, Mrs Smith, was a cousin of the burly Tom Clough, canal dredger and our Sunday School superintendent.

My parents also had to carry their midday food with them. My mother used a cloth bag; my father carried his break in a handkerchief. At first I too had a cloth bag which I hung up in the inner porch at the school until I found that mice, running up the coats, had anticipated my dinner and left me only a small portion. After that I carried a metal box with a handle such as was commonly carried by the mill workers. We ate our lunch in the porch or, when the weather was fine, standing about in the yard.

At home, before we had gas and a gas-ring I could kindle a fire with wood, a supply of which was never short as my father brought fragments of broken corves and oddments from the joiner's floor every day. My task was made easy by the warmth and even a glow in the grate not yet cold after the boiling of water for my parents' drink.

I made myself a drink of cocoa ('Broma' cocoa from the Co-op), tea being drunk only at teatime on Saturday and Sunday, when there was a tablecloth and my mother liked a bit of fuss over the meal. We never had coffee.

Tea (the meal) which I had when my father came home was like my breakfast, but we had the supplementary meal of tripe or cowheel on the appropriate night, and on baking night there was rice pudding. My mother made several little puddings, which stood for a time on top of the oven, adjacent to my father's feet which were always up there for most of the evening.

On baking nights I had to go to Farrer's farm "on t' common" for an extra quart of milk. Normally we had only a pint delivered from the milkman's open can. My mother put butter, sugar and egg in the rice puddings and the anticipation used to make me run up Kitson Hill on choir practice nights to look straight at the oven top to see if a pudding had come out to stand there, warm and ready. She was also good at making sponge loaves, a treat for the weekend. In holiday time some rice pudding left over from the night before was a quickly warmed-up meal.

In those periods also I used to boil some potatoes and eat a large quantity lubricated with butter or dripping. I occasionally fried potato collops and onions, in such unwise quantity that I was distended before completing the feast.

On Pancake Tuesday it was the custom to stuff ourselves tight with a series of pancakes done in fat brought to fuming point and then served with a thick smearing of treacle. The next pouring of batter followed into the pan immediately on the exit of the one before, and so on till the bowl of batter had been scraped out clean into the pan. It was a busy operation, eating one pancake and watching the frying-pan at the same time for the moment to try to get the knife under the pancake to see whether it had sufficient consistency for lifting and turning over. I have seen my mother attempt the tossing of a pancake. She could on rare occasions be sufficiently light-hearted as to dare to attempt such a thing, but this was very risky with a pancake. My father's wrath at an error would have cost us a miserable time.

Weekends

The climax of the week, the weekend, was a time to look forward to. The Friday upheaval for cleaning was over, floor and windows washed. Rugs were back in their places and chairs down off the table and, by tea-time, dusting was done and a visit to the Co-op made. My mother used to bring back some cheese and sometimes a malt loaf. A special treat also was a bag of nuts, which I now know as barcelona nuts. My father used to crack these by putting two together in his hand. I also acquired this knack. We had no nut-crackers.

My mother liked the approach to the Saturday tea and the tea on Sunday too. She used to keep the table covered with a precious damask patterned material. At the time for bringing on the things, she would fold this half back, leaving room for a white table-cloth, this coming out only on Saturday and Sunday for teatime, when this extra trouble happened to be taken. The *Yorkshire Evening Post* had sufficed for the rest of the week. We had a set of china cups and saucers, and teaspoons were brought out of the table drawer. The tinkle of these in the saucers was part of the ceremony. Tea (a change from the weekday cocoa), malt loaf, cheese, and perhaps some celery made a feast, completed sometimes with a bit of sponge loaf made on baking night.

The Sunday dinner was appetising, too, beginning with the Yorkshire pudding, served at the start, hot from the large tin, always light and puffy and unfailingly browned to the right, beautiful degree. Rich gravy freshly made from the meat and poured from the gravy boat initiated this delicious course. The best meal of the week, it never varied. The pudding was followed by peas and mashed potato, to which was added some meat. The joint was always put by my father's plate. My mother used to get some for herself but what I was to have was torn off by hand and passed to my plate by my father. My mother sometimes said: "Nay, gi' t'lad a bit moor:" My father wished to make sure that there would be some meat left over to put in his teacake for Monday's dinner. I used to watch his thumb, thickened with manual work and with dirt ingrained.

Years later, after he had retired, I was astonished at the change in the appearance of his hands. In all my childhood and youth I had never seen them so white.

It was a pity that the Sunday time was so often chosen by my father for a particularly emphatic homily on my idleness and uselessness, and my unawareness of the debt of gratitude I owed him. I owed everything to him. When he toiled in dirt and darkness, foul air and danger in the pit bottom, I was doing nothing at home or sitting looking at books at school - and what did I know? "Nought, not an inch o't rooad but we s'ud see". I should either be a man or a mouse. My tears spoiled my appetite and I envied my classmates in the Elementary School who had gone to work half-time or full-time as soon as possible.

I should like to have been able to talk about my studies to my father, but his education had been slight, and he was not inclined to go along with me in learning. He was confident that 'he knew'. One Saturday dinnertime I did broach the subject of the solar system, and referred to the high temperature of the sun. My father bluntly said "Nowt o't sooart: As yer go oop an' oop yer get co'der an' co'der, an' if yer were pressed oop ageean t'sun yeed be frozen to deeath!"

Not long after I became a choir boy there was one of the occasional visits to our house by some people we had formerly known in the Bradford area; I cannot remember who they were. Such visits stopped. There was a reference to my singing and my father ordered me to sing. I was nervous and reluctant. He said "Sing, or I'll knock t'aup side o' yer heead off!" So there followed my attempt to sing through my tears the hymn I knew best then, a favourite of our old headmaster, *The day thou gavest, Lord, is ended*, while the visitors listened, embarrassed.

Once when my father had gone out after putting me in my place I went upstairs brooding at his treatment of me and wishing I could be out of it. When my mother came up she saw I was upset, and I exclaimed: "My father does not love me!" This was the only time that that word was used of any relationship among us three. My mother corrected me, saying: "You're the apple of his eye". She must have told my father what I had said, for the next time my father and I were together he stared, silent and unfrowning, at me.

In my last year at the university, which I spent back in residence at home, I became so worried about failure and the fear of proving my father's forecast about my uselessness that, at Easter, I ventured to assure him that I had tried as well as I knew how and, if I failed, I would go to the Labour Exchange. The introduction of this institution, and my discovery as to where there was an office, gave me courage and hope that I might be able to 'stop wasting my time' and 'owing everything'.

Indiscretions

In my teens in holiday time I once experimented with a recipe. A workmate of my mother's, a frequenter of the Baptist Chapel, persuaded her to buy a copy of a recipe-and-proverb book being sold for fund raising. I attempted a ginger pudding in a steamer on the fire. By that time we had a double pan, and my father had taken a fancy to an occasional supper of Quaker Oats porridge. I prepared the ingredients and stood them in a pot in the steamer, but there was an error in the recipe or I misread it, for the pudding rose so much that it came over the side of the pot, into the steamer, raised the pan lid and oozed down into the fire. There was some left in the pot for my dinner, but I did not go on with such experiments for fear of having to risk censure for my wasteful muddling.

In holiday time when I had been playing with the Holmeses in the morning, we would separate for dinner. The 'whew' (hooter) at Godfrey Walker's mill reminded us of the time, and I went home for my solitary meal. I ventured to ask whether Harry Holmes, a hunchback, rather older than me, could bring his dinner and eat with me. I liked Harry. In spite of the sharp angle in his spine he did his best to take part in our play. This hampered our vigour and we had been brought to a worried pause because he had burst into tears in the pain of being accidentally jolted. One day it happened that my mother, having 'felled out' early, came home before Harry had gone. I was terrified when she walked in, for fear she should tell my father when he returned, but I think she read my thoughts, and was discreet. I never risked having a guest again. No children crossed our doorstep when my father was at home.

Another indiscretion had occurred when I was very young. Others of my age came to play on our flags and we talked wildly about Indians till we got the idea of making a camp fire. This we did with some of our firewood on the stone floor before the hearth. Fortunately we had left the door open and a woman neighbour passing heard our din and came to look. She soon had us and the fire under control. I was lucky again. Probably, knowing my father, she did not dare talk about our mischief, at any rate not carelessly.

For those days my father's return at tea-time was early, and I always felt fear increasing as five o'clock approached. In holiday time I used to loiter at our gate and look down the hill for the figure turning the corner with the characteristic lump on one side where the wood was partially concealed. There was too much not to render it obvious what was there. I had to be ready to receive my father, who would drop the wood and flop down in his chair for me to take his boots off. They smelt of mud and oil, of which they had a permanent, thick coating. An additional smell came from the thick stockings. My father washed himself, apart from his face, only at the weekend, and then not thoroughly, so that the combination of smells, especially in summer was nauseating as I knelt at his feet.

My father's humour varied from ominous silence to rough scolding, but I usually succeeded in getting through the time up to my mother's return by quiet submission. There was the meal to think about and on baking night I could go up to the farm for the quart of milk.

On Fridays we had the fireside to attend to. We had a pit in front of the fire into which the ashes dropped after the coal-rake had pulled the droppings from the fire over the covering grate. The larger ashes were reserved to make a foundation for the next fire, being stored on the brick shelf behind the fire. It was my job to carry the ashes round to the ashpit (midden) at the far end of the garden of the house behind and adjacent to the dry closet we shared with that house.

While I was doing that my father was doing the blackleading of the bars of the fire grate and the tip-up flap where we rested pans. A paste was made with the blacklead and water and applied with a brush. When that was dry another brush was needed for polishing. I did this when I was older.

In this teatime period when I was still quite a small boy my father got the whim to make me pretend to spar with him. He must have been remembering the days when as a lad he boxed with Herbert Slater (who married my Aunt Martha) in a quiet part of the park at Low Moor. We had a constant reminder in a photo of the two with fists up, over the steps leading to our little cellar. My father sat in his chair and I stood in front of him making timid thrusts towards his face. This sham business came to an abrupt end one afternoon when a flush of sadism came over him and he dealt me a blow on the jaw which sent me staggering back dizzy and crying.

As time went on I reached an age when most of my contemporaries at the Elementary school were out earning. I was at the Grammar School, and schooling was not regarded by my father as work. Only manual effort was worthy of that word.

The long school holidays were a trying time and increased my father's annoyance at my idleness. Circumstances were difficult. Attempts had to be made to account for the use of time when I was on holiday. There was only little I could say at teatime, such as more tabs put in if we were making a rug, a bird or animal or human face copied in ink, and some practice on the violin done, which I disliked and did to a minimum extent. More useful would be a pair of boots mended. I had at first watched my father repairing boots or clogs and made attempts when quite young to mend my own footwear.

I had little idea as to what I could do to help my progress towards certainty of getting a job later. There was little I could study. There was no guidance at school, and no public library. For holidays there was only a small cupboardful at the Grammar School from which the English mistress allowed us to take a book home. I had no contact with anyone who had gone my way before me. In any case reading gave me nothing to show my father at five o'clock.

After the violin came I could say I had done some practice and I attempted to have something to show by copying a face out of a newspaper or book. My father continued to tell me I had never done an hour's work in my life even after I had returned from the war, but I made bold to describe some things we had had to do there and he was quiet for a while. But he returned to his old contempt as I went on with my studies.

Tasks

Certain activities, one of them regular, gave me something to show my father. It was my job from time-to-time when I returned from the Copleys' to make firewood out of the lumps which my father daily brought home.. I did this in the coalplace if the coal was low enough, otherwise on the flags near the coalplace door. For this work my father had made a hatchet of a design I have never seen elsewhere, hammer on one side and curved axe-edge opposite, with the handle made from a pick-shaft. I was inexpert at first and one day I struck my left forefinger next to the joint with the hand, knocking up a flap of skin. Mrs Crawshaw next door was at home and I went there. There is still a faint mark on my finger.

Not all the wood was made into small firewood for kindling and early morning quick boiling for cocoa. Some of it was exceedingly hard and knotty and had to be broken with a cold chisel, for putting under the oven or under the fireside boiler on Monday nights for the washing.

Our rugs were home-made. Two kinds of material were used for fixing to the canvas, both coming from my mother's mill. She brought healds, an arrangement like short strings on a long string. These were sewn on to the canvas and used for the bedroom floor. The other kind of rug was made with tabs or 'lists', and required a heavy wooden frame to stretch the canvas and a beam for rolling up the rug as it progressed. My father made two prickers of iron so that two workers could operate side by side. The tabs were made from fents (waste fabric) brought home by my mother. Learoyd's made very good cloth, worsted, some for officers' uniforms, and we got excellent samples in brilliant red as well as blues and blacks and greens. We became expert at pricking and I have spent hours in holiday time during the day for my father to compare progress from the place where work was left the night before. There was an interest in planning the pattern and studying how to make that fit the fents obtained. The rugs thus made were so heavy that it took two of us bent double at the shaking out on the road on Friday nights. The canvas eventually gave way under the strain. My father had to give up shaking as the weight and the violent tugging were too much for him. My mother continued with my help when I was strong enough.

An occasional task for me was to clean the brass canary cage. My father was interested in two extras: an enormous aspidistra, next to a fern on the window bottom; and the canary in the cage suspended over the chest of drawers next to the window. It was in the holidays that I dealt with the cage, cleaning the brass with metal polish, including the wires, wiping them carefully because the bird used to wipe its beak on them and the perches. More frequently I had to attend to the two cups slotted in at the ends for water and food, as well as cleaning the tray at the bottom.

My Yorkshire Folk in the Early 1900s

My father wanted to have a canary but he did nothing with it or for it. However, he took some trouble about getting a good singer. Canary keeping seems to have been one of the miners' hobbies. I went once with my father four miles to a cottage opposite the Walton Cross. The remaining stump of this is in a field a few yards from the road running past Hartshead Church, associated with the Reverend Patrick Brontë. We were taken upstairs to a room full of cages and a cheerful cacophonous chirping. Another time we walked even further, along Windy Bank Lane, where another miner bred canaries. On these occasions I heard talk about Norwich canaries and German rollers. Perhaps they had been brought in earlier by weavers who had crossed over from the Low Countries during the hand-loom weaving days, first in East Anglia and then coming to the West Riding mills.

We had two cages – an old one into which I put the bird for cleaning the good cage and for giving it a shower. For that there was a metal tube with a part connected with a bracket so as to leave a gap. Fitting the tube with its cork into a bottleneck, I blew hard and the suction drew up water which issued as a spray over the bird. It did not like the process. Perhaps my father was mistaken in thinking it necessary to wash the bird.

Another occasional task was housing our load of coals. Colliers were entitled to one 'coal-note' per month, ie permission for a free ton of coal, but they had to pay for transport. Coal could be obtained from 'Blaggy's' (Blackburn's). The continuation of Kitson Hill Road is called Lea Green and the two Blackburn brothers had a couple of horses stabled down there. These horses pulled the heavy, large-wheeled tip-up cart, such as was commonly used by farmers for taking manure to the fields or bringing in turnips. The regular work of the Blackburn men and horses was the journey to and fro between the Three Nuns Pit and the gasworks at Ravensthorpe. (The gasworks and the Grammar School were the only joint enterprises between Mirfield and our neighbour.) Any intervals between loads required left the cart and horses free to be hired by a collier.

My father used to get a note from some collier who had been unable to keep up with his monthly free tons. Transport was my father's only expense. This was five shillings. The coal used to be tipped in the road against our coalplace. Till I was strong enough to wield the big shovel my father would house the coal at the end of the day. During the day if I was at home, I got in what I could with the bucket (a wooden one, made of staves bound with hoops, and obtained from the Co-op from where it had come full of lard). As soon as I was big enough I got the coal in myself, having it all to throw up to the hole in the wall. I felt happier on those days for 'having done an hour's work'.

A task which came round each autumn followed the delivery of a sack of potatoes fresh from the field. Abel Buck's father was a farmhand on land attached to a big house down Lea Green about three quarters of a mile from our house, and we had an arrangement for a hundredweight each autumn. We had little room in the house and the potatoes were coated with moist soil as they had just been lifted We had to empty them on our stone floor downstairs under the table and spent much time wiping them before leaving them to dry. Then they were transferred to our one room upstairs and spread again under my parents' bed to continue to dry. After some days they were moved once more to a large tub in the coalplace to be covered with a sack and brought out as required. Bread and mashed potato being our staple diet, we consumed a considerable quantity each week. The coalplace was damp and we found we had to move the remaining potatoes back again to the bedroom floor, with some loss in rotten ones. Potatoes were regarded as so essential that all this trouble was worthwhile.

There was a weekly routine of evening work at our house. Monday night was washing night, Wednesday baking (later moved to Thursday), Friday cleaning. On baking night, when my mother had had her tea and recovered a little from the hard work at the mill and the long walk, she emptied out the poke of flour I had fetched from the Co-op. It went into a large earthenware bowl warming on the fender. My father and I had already heated the oven with wood and coal, and I had fetched the extra quart of milk from Farrer's farm. Yeast, milk and warm water poured into a depression in the middle of the flour began to bubble up. At a certain stage a cloth over the bowl was removed and the formation of the dough began. When it was firm enough, the bowl was lifted down onto the floor and my mother knelt down and began pulling it in from the sides and pummelling it with clenched fists. Taking the mass of dough to a baking board on the table, she cut sections for fitting into loaf tins or for rolling-out into 'oven-bottom cakes'. Loaf tins and cake tins were arranged on the fender for further rising in front of the fire before being put into the oven. The bread was always perfectly baked, which was remarkable considering the difficulty of maintaining adequate even heat in an oven heated by coal.

There were evenings when the work was not so hard and my mother did a little ironing, particularly of my father's starched collar and front for when he wished to go out on a Saturday or Sunday evening. This neck-and-front wear was stiff and uncomfortable, and there was much fumbling with studs at the front and the back of the neck. The ironing was done at first with a block of iron heated in the fire and placed in the holder with tongs, a method replaced later, but unsatisfactorily, with a charcoal iron. This was a failure because of the difficulty of kindling and maintaining the glow, and sometimes smuts of dirt escaped from the funnel.

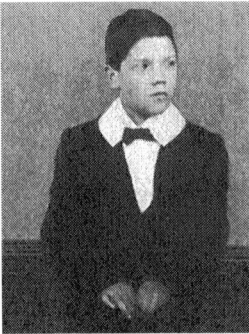

There was no ironing to be done for me, as my collars were of composition and could be washed with soap and water. I hated the discomfort at the neck of those high, stiff collars and was glad when I passed to collar-attached shirts. In those days smartness and discomfort were too often associated.

There was another, lighter, evening job before the weekend effort began on Friday. Plenty of stocking mending awaited my mother's 'leisure' time. We walked a great deal and woollen stockings soon wore into holes, but mending them was a job she could do sitting down.

My Yorkshire Folk in the Early 1900s

On Friday nights my mother made a great to-do about cleaning, washing the stone house floor, the guillotine (sash) windows (sitting riskily half-in half-out of the windows upstairs) and the flags outside up to the edge of the road. 'Ruddling' was a matter of pride with her. Down on her knees she rubbed the yellow, soft stone (ruddle) on the edges, with a rim of white. The window bottoms outside were also ruddled. During road excavations in Mirfield Moor a large quantity of this soft stone was lifted up and I went with my cart for loads of it. My mother's Friday night work was carried on in the dark sometimes, the house door being open and the curtains undrawn. On Fridays I would be off to the Co-op, though she herself would be there also on the Saturday afternoon.

By Saturday teatime my mother could ease off a little, but not until the oil lamp suspended over the table had been taken down. The charred wick had to be brushed clear, the funnel washed, the globe washed and the container filled with paraffin. For this I was sent up the hill with a big can to a hut where, as a side-line, a carter stored a variety of household necessities: candles, tapers, brushes, firelighters and low quality soft soap.

In my early years, if my father had gone to a neighbouring town on the Saturday afternoon, my mother would sometimes for a change, when everything seemed to be done, sit me in my infant's chair (with its hole and lid) and read a little for me while I sat beside her on my tuffet. I had received as prizes for attendance at Sunday School two or three simple books of idealistic anecdotes.

Joseph H Hird

My mother's reading effort could not last long. As she had gone to the mill to work half-time at the age of ten and done no reading since, the mental effort was too much for her tired brain, and she lapsed into a sleep which I carefully avoided disturbing.

I cannot recall all that without great admiration for my mother's energy, but I wish she had taken more care of herself and less of the house. If she had been less of a slave to the house routine, she could have reduced much of her activity; but with a kind of masochism she seemed to think she acquired merit by her slavish activity.

Also the neighbours could see that she was 'a clean woman'.

Battyeford Co-op

It was on her return from the Co-op one Saturday afternoon that I first heard of Boy Scouts. A boy in that uniform had come up to my mother as she was coming up the fields and insisted on taking her bag. He explained why he was doing this. It was his 'good turn' for that day. He got an orange for his trouble.

I spent much time on Friday nights or Saturday afternoons at Battyeford Co-op. There was a very slow manager, Harry Schofield, who spent most of his time at his desk behind the big biscuit-tin frame, leaving the serving to his assistant, Harold Chilton. Much of the food had to be weighed out as demanded: butter, lard, bacon, sugar, treacle, flour, potatoes. Butter and lard came in bulk, in large wooden tubs. These, when inverted, dumped the great mass on to the counter. A long piece of wire with handles was

140

used to pull through them at a convenient depth. The two wooden spatulas detached a block of the approximate weight. The shopman slapped and patted the lump to make a regular shaped block for wrapping. There had to be double wrapping with paper to contain the grease. Transferred to the brass scales, beautiful, shining works of art, with an accompanying row of graduated weights, like little dollies, the block suffered more paring or addition and more slapping until the two scale pans came level. This weighing was one of the things schoolboys were put on to on leaving school. I met some of them at it and while I watched the treatment we renewed our acquaintance as former Elementary School classmates. Such a boy was known as a 'butter-slapper'.

For the treacle, used for little else than to mix with flowers of sulphur for blood purification, I had an earthenware jar. This received two weighings, one empty and another after the filling, under a pipe which ran down the wall behind the counter from the tank on the floor above. There could not be an adjustment for quantity this time, so the assistant made an estimate according to the weight he had used.

My father required a weekly supply of 'thick twist'. There was a long black coil of this at the shop. Again there was an estimate, for it was not suitable to cut bits off to take back. Success in a shop lad's training showed in the degree of precision attained in these estimates. Familiarity sometimes made an estimate exact. In the evening and at the weekend, my father cut off a portion of twist with the sharp knife which he used for cutting leather when cobbling, and then rubbed it up between his hands.

Joseph H Hird

The bulky bins for flour and potatoes were in a back room. I took an old bag for the potatoes, but for flour I had a cloth poke, getting a stone at a time. This white bag had a cover to fold and tie over it. I carried this load home on my head, as well as two bags in my hands. In my pocket I brought home a quantity of metal cheques of nominal value equal to the amount spent.

With goods gradually accumulated after much walking to and fro round the circumference of the shop, Harold arranged the objects in a line and placed his hand on each one in turn from left to right while doing mental arithmetic. It was impossible to follow what he was adding, with his temporary totals and repetitions, but every one accepted his jabber, no demand being made for any visible evidence. When the total had been arrived at, he turned round to a box containing tin cheques corresponding to pounds, shilling and pence. He then spread out the quantity to which one was entitled. In those days wages were slow in rising to a pound a week, so that silver and copper sufficed for shopping. Paper money for low denominations had not yet come into the hands of working people, and I saw no paper money at all. (A certain Friday night came when my father received his first golden sovereign: he put it on the table and turned it over for us to admire.)

It occurred to the Battyeford Co-op committee later that there was a simpler way of assessing the dividend than handing out tin cheques, and the paper cheque came into use. I joined the queue on the periodical Saturday afternoons to get the 'divi', careful reckoning having been done at home with the filed cheques to avoid error. These paper chits were a great improvement on the mass of metal tokens we used to keep in a stone jar and whose return to the shop and recalculation imposed an additional and tedious task on the assistant.

The lengthy process of shopping might be supposed to have caused impatience amongst customers waiting their turn. Not at all. Few men went shopping, and on Friday evening or Saturday afternoon, women came in and met their usual acquaintances. There was a bench placed in front of the counters and the shelves extending all round the room, and in winter a coke stove maintained a pleasant temperature. Pushing their shawls back over their shoulders the women began the exchange of news and comment. As one woman moved to the counter, the other women moved up and a newcomer could then find room at the other end. The news could then start again, with an expectation of new details and comments. Husbands decided that the Co-op was a 'reight call oil' (a real taking shop).

The Co-ops had started as a working class movement and remained such. No 'nice people' went there. They sent for the groceries to the private enterprise shops.

9

Washing, Clothes and Sanitation

With the Monday evening washing activities there was much exertion required. We had a heavy wooden tub with a peggy, a wooden device like a stool with four legs and a rod sticking up from the middle with a crosspiece at the top to permit a vigorous twisting to and fro. A later development was the posser, a large copper cup shape on the end of a shaft, the motion with this being up and. down. There were slits in the sides of the copper fitting through which air and water were forced by the lift and down thrust. The suction was expected to draw the dirt out. This article was lighter than the all-wooden peggy but it could be tiring.

The tub stood in front of the mangle, so that the water could run back into it. The process of mangling was entirely my job. The heavy wooden rollers were turned with a set of gears activated by the large wheel with hand grip at right angles. Again modernisation improved this process by the invention of thin, rubber rollers, but they were delicate and allowed the rubber to come loose if too much pressure was tightened down on the wormed shafts leading to the springs at the ends of the rollers.

We had a large three-legged pan with a long handle for boiling clothes over the fire (my father's clothes, in particular, became very dirty). This vessel was called a *posnet*. It was much too big for the space above the fire and projected forward from the flat hinged top of the ribs. It was ready for my mother to start the washing as soon as she would have had her tea.

I made a drawing of this for art homework once and the art master, Mr Pearson, burst out laughing at the funny object and the funnier name.

For our posnet my father asked the joiner at the pit to make a thick wooden lid, to the middle of which my father fixed a handle of his forging. The lid warped with use. My mother could just manage to lift the posnet off the fire on to the side of the hearth to wait for the next process.

On one occasion (this happened before I was three and was sent to the Copleys'), I stood on the lid with my right foot to reach up to some scissors on a hook above. The warped lid tilted and in went my foot. It was badly scalded. My mother got me on to a chair and awaited my father's homecoming. I remember the occasion well. My father would not have any outside assistance. No doctor ever came to our house while I lived with my parents. He bathed and wrapped up the foot, and in time I could use it again. Scars still cover the top of my right foot.

Clothes were dried by being hung on strings across from beam to beam above the hearth. These strings were seldom empty. We used steps to reach ours.

Aunt Rose had an improved arrangement, a frame which could be lowered, and she used hers also for drying havercakes, sheets of oatmeal cake which were hawked soft.

Clothes

For footwear from early childhood up to going to the Grammar School I wore clogs on weekdays and boots on Sundays, never shoes. The clogs had thick wooden soles with brass toe-caps and irons. These irons were shaped to the under edge of the soles and heels and punctured with holes in a groove for nailing. To make the irons last longer, my father used to level up the space between with leather brought from the pit. This he called 'bucket leather' from its use on the pistons which drew up the water from the pit sump. The wear on the buckets was heavy and we always had a supply at home of parts of those discarded. Repairs of clogs and boots were done at home, and in due course I became 'apprenticed' to this work.

Clogs could be obtained either new as such or by conversion from boots. When a conversion was needed I used to go to the clogger's on Eastthorpe (*the road pictured below*) and watch him at work. He worked in a room so small that he could reach nearly everything he needed without rising. There was hardly room to sit while waiting. Waiting was not tedious. He talked pleasantly and down to my level, working without interruption by the light of the fanlike flame of a naked gas jet, and seldom raising his

eyes. A large proportion of the congested tools and materials was in the shadows, but he knew just where everything was.

Clogs were warm and dry and could look smart when repeatedly polished. If bought as clogs rather than converted boots they tended to have stiff sides and the top edge could be unkind to the anklebones. They were cheaper to buy and easier to repair than boots. It was possible for us boys to indulge in making sparks as we ran down the causeway in the dark winter, by swinging a foot round smartly to strike a glancing blow at the stone flags. I used to try to control this temptation because of the risk of dislocating an iron. but I could not keep out of it when the whim to do this occurred to boys with whom I happened to be.

When a fight took place the narrow, metal-capped toes of the heavy clogs made an opponent's feet much more dangerous than his hands.

The noise of our marching into the Elementary School was as near thunderous as we dared to make it and led, in some really immoderate cases, to being sent back to march round the porch again. We did not walk straight forward into the long room from the yard, but had to march round an old umbrella stand at the far end.

For the services at church on Sundays, clogs were out of the question; the quiet solemnity could not have been maintained with the sound of clog irons on the tiled floors. Clogs would have been inconsistent with the idea of wearing Sunday best for church. In fact it was the church which decided when new clothes should be worn. The occasion was Whit Sunday, and on that day at morning school boys eyed each other to see what other parents had chosen. The interest was not at all less when the girls came over from the Nab School, where they had had their morning classes, to proceed up the aisle to their allotted places.

My father himself turned to boots for his work. I do not know why, unless it was better cover for the ankles. The mud and oil along the rail tracks in the pit bottom would have been resisted better by clogs. It was leather-laced boots I used to kneel to on his return. They were never scraped clean, but he liked the contrast at the weekend of a well polished pair of boots.

For people who did not do their own boot repairs as my father did, the cobblers were kept busy, as there was much walking. The soles and heels of a workman's boots were strongly reinforced with nails, iron rims for the heels and iron tips for the toes. For men above labouring status, walking was less noisy due to a revolving rubber heel secured with a central screw.

During one period boot repairing was the occupation of two men, Herbert and Leonard Walker both living in houses behind ours. They shared a shed for work in Eastthorpe.

Before that happened, the younger brother, Leonard, had taken a wooden shed in a field not far from our church. I went there sometimes on errands with neighbours' boots, and saw him at work All the apparatus and all the work could be seen from the counter. Sheets of hides were suspended. There was a hole in the top of a stout, wooden stump for the insertion of the particular last for the size of boot. The boot was held firm with a rope passed across the instep and kept rigid by the cobbler's foot passed through a loop. He had a rapid technique for fixing a sole. Having put in a couple of nails to hold it in place, he threw a small handful of nails into his mouth and started a rhythmical 1-2-3 time: 1, left hand up to take the nail pushed forward ready by the tongue and brought down to the spot on the sole; 2, a gentle tap with the big file used instead of a hammer; 3, a heavy blow settling the nail. The cycle of movements took about two seconds. It is astonishing that Leonard carried on for years with this insanitary habit.

For boys' leg-covering there was an intermediate stage between the short trousers exposing the knees, and long trousers. Up to the age of about sixteen we had breeches which fastened with a tab and button under the knee, and this fastening was often concealed with what were called cycling stockings

having the top turned down and embroidered.

I think we passed symbolically to young manhood rather earlier than the girls made the corresponding change. For them this was indicated by 'putting their hair up', ie changing from pigtail or tress tied with a bow to a method of twisting and stowing the hair behind the head, the technique of securing with hairpins having to be learnt. I do not think any girl would have dared to do this before she left the Grammar School. There, we boys had progressed from breeches to trousers by the time we reached Form Six in the fourth year.

I had cotton lined trousers and no underpants. This latter garment was not acquired till I went to the war. Trousers became a clammy, unpleasant thing, being never washed in my case, though my father's thick, fustian trousers did get a wash on rare occasions. The expression *body odour* was unknown to us, but the thing was a familiar fact.

Clothes provided for me were a mixture of new and second-hand. My mother also made our shirts out of flannel, with the treadle sewing-machine. She was not well practised in such work, but the economy effected induced her to try her best.

My father heard of a second hand clothes shop in Halifax to which we made an occasional journey, walking to Brighouse and then riding on the tram via Hove Edge, Hipperholme and the cutting at Godley Lane, places with which I was to become familiar much later. The walls and bench in the clothes shop were loaded with a confusion of garments, turned over and over by anyone wanting a bargain. There were some well-wearing things to be had, descended from 'the better sort'. For example, we got for me an overcoat for half a crown made from good material. It was of anticipatory size and my hands were out of sight. I passed the curate one day; he gave me a sympathetic halfpenny. I was doing an errand at the time and was only thirty yards from Mellor's sweets shop at the bottom of the Nab. I soon made a conversion to sweets. I did not wear the jacket much, but it was useful for putting on the bed.

One trip to Halifax has fixed for me the date of the death of Florence Nightingale. As we emerged into the centre of the town we saw the posters for the evening newspaper and heard the newsvendors crying the event. It was the year 1910.

Sanitation

The system of sanitation of those days had habituated us to foul smells. We shared a dry closet with the house behind ours. We made the journey under observation, in winter taking a candle and lighting it when we had closed the door to keep out the wind. The stink when we raised the lid before going into session became more and more overpowering as the weeks went by up to the time when the night-soil men came. Then the shovelling out and piling up at the side of the house informed the whole neighbourhood.

The clearing out had two stages: the midden outside first, containing ashes and any other rubbish and then, via the midden, the human deposit, approached through a connecting hole at the side of the closet. All this material was transferred by wheel barrow to be dumped at the side of the house, so that when the cart returned from taking away the previous load, it and successive piles from adjacent property could be loaded. Midden, closet and pile having been cleared, some pinkish powder, carbolic I think, was emptied into a bucket from a sack and scattered on the three places. The change of smell was welcome and gave us the impression that our Urban District Council was paying due regard to health.

There were other inconveniences connected with this early kind of sanitation. We made the journey round the side of the house and along the garden path behind only for bowel action, with our piece of newspaper, of which any spare was left in the 'nessy', as it was called. It was useful often for the wiping of the seat which had to be done before one could act. For bladder emptying, the vessel upstairs was used and emptied into a sink over a drain which ran in front of our house, only about a yard from the door and in our own garden.

It frequently happened that the journey round the back was futile because there was an occupant from the house behind. We had to return to the house, wondering when it might be safe to repeat the journey. There was a system for knowing if someone was coming when one was inside. A little round hole in the door enabled a finger to be put through for lifting the wooden latch. One could look through and give a cough when the visitor was thought to be near enough, putting up a foot against the door meanwhile in case the cough had not been heard.

The system was more difficult in the dark. One hoped the little circle of light and line of light at the edge of the door would be noticed. But not everybody kept a light all the time, as taking a candle was a nuisance in windy and wet weathers In those conditions we struck a match, having firmly shut the door, took a quick look at the situation, and proceeded in darkness.

It is not to be wondered at that, along with the unsuitable diet, constipation was a constant hindrance to good tone of health. In a cupboard in our sideboard were two jars side by side, one for flowers of sulphur and one for treacle (dark). On Sundays my mother made a mixture of which I took a tablespoonful. This medicine was called treacle-and-brimstone.

In my boyhood and youth I used to have a bilious attack about once every three months, no doubt due to my diet. Once at the age of eight I had been very sick in school and was sent home. I carried a house-key, of course, from the time I left Copleys' at eight years, a big key filling all the bottom of my jacket pocket. I managed to get upstairs and lie on the bed where I was found in the evening. When my mother came home from the mill I felt grateful for her remark that if she had known she would have broken off her work. She said this discreetly to me upstairs. Stopping work would, of course, have delayed felling out (finishing weaving the piece), and so losing money. What she said was unique, the only occasion during the whole of the time I knew her that she said anything suggesting affection.

One of these bilious attacks occurred most unfortunately later, when the choirmaster, Mr Gadsby, had invited me to take my violin to his house. He took me upstairs where I made one of my earliest acquaintanceships with indoor sanitation.

It was understood that my mother and the woman at the back, whoever she happened to be (there were several changes of rear neighbours) should take turns at washing the closet. Some of the back-to-back neighbours were lazy and there were arguments. A time came after I had left Kitson Hill, when my parents stopped using the closet. All the washing of it had been left to my mother who always found the place in a disgusting condition. My father went across the road and climbed over into the plantation belonging to Fieldhead estate and my mother got permission to use a neighbour's place.

During my time at home the closet became very unpleasant. My mother's scrubbing of the floor had, in time, washed away the lime joining the flags, and liquid oozed out from under the seat. This was a feast for the flies which normally confined their feeding and reproduction to the midden and the hole under the seat which was covered with a round lid with handle on top.

The floor reached a state when the nicks between the flags were a seething mass of maggots. My father obtained some cement from the pit and pointed the gaps thoroughly, successfully confining those loathsome things to the place where they could repeat their life cycle without forcing our attention too closely on their activity.

There was plentiful dung about our neighbourhood, not only as above, but as horse droppings on the road in front of the house. The huge heaps outside the farms and the spread of this manure on the fields within a few yards of us produced a pest of flies in summer. There was a less offensive side, however. I used to go up and down the road with bucket and shovel, and often had a full supply for the garden within a few yards. I could easily have obtained sufficient for a garden far bigger than our couple of square yards, in which we grew lettuce and a little mustard.

On Sunday mornings in summer while I was at church my mother would be busy cooking meat and potatoes and peas, to be preceded by Yorkshire pudding with gravy. I approached the house with mouth moist with anticipation of this once-a-week cooked hot meal. At this season the flies, attracted by the same smell from the open door, invaded the house and led to a hunt. We had a strap handy and I was soon busy slapping surfaces all over the house. The enemy often escaped us as it was inadvisable to slap too hard on wallpaper. Better places were the huge stone over the fireplace, the door jambs, the cupboard door and the two beams along the ceiling. My father would come down from his morning nap sometimes and take over, but he could not jump up as well as I could. I scored fifty sometimes between return from church and my mother's welcome interruption.

10

My Money-making Ventures

I had no pocket-money from my parents but was not penniless. I ran errands, for example to the butcher's, three quarters of a mile away and to a corner shop for tobacco for the boilerman at the currier's mill. I have helped on occasion to turn the handle of the cutting wheel with the sharp blades for making 'choppy' of hay, and for cutting up turnips.

The limitation of my private funds encouraged an attitude of care in the way in which I spent my money. Annually in the summer a fair came to the centre of Mirfield. I remember wandering all round it, with my hand on the tuppence I had brought. I left the fairground after contemplating all the attractions, with my tuppence still intact.

During my last three years at the Elementary School I sold newspapers on Saturday mornings. It had happened that one day during Mr Greenwood's lesson in the porch, when I was standing on the form in the back line, Tom Wood whispered to me asking whether I would like to sell newspapers. I asked him to wait till playtime. I got details and mentioned the matter at home. There were three newsagents in Mirfield, all on Eastthorpe. I started at Rogers' at sixpence (6d).

I rose with my parents on Saturdays now. I had to go to the newspaper shop, about a mile and a half away, get the cart and go with other boys to Mirfield station to wait for the train from Dewsbury. We liked the business of riding with the cart up the lift which was worked by water. One had to pull hard on an iron rod which extended all the way up the shaft. The guards-van would be wide open by the time the train approached, and we liked to be clever and jump in while the train was still in motion, to help throw out the bundles. There was no adult with us. One boy, Harry Wood, Tom's brother, once had his foot trapped in the space between the side of the lift and the wall.

In connection with the newspaper job my father pleased me by having a cart made. I was keen to have a cart and had taken much trouble about finding a certain boy one Saturday afternoon at a football match and trying to persuade him to sell me a pair of pram wheels which I had heard he had. It came to nothing; to get rid of me he had hardly deigned to turn his eyes away from the game. My father procured a pair of wheels from the pit over which the rope passed for pulling the corves in the pit bottom. These had grooved rims, and my father fitted iron tyres and made axles, the woodwork being supplied by the joiner at the opposite end of the workshop. I was very proud of this cart, which we managed to squeeze into the coalplace. On Saturday mornings I pushed it along the causeway with a pleasant din and clatter as it bumped from flag to flag.

Joseph H Hird

I left Rogers' after a row. We were put on various rounds, in pairs at times and my last companion was a jolly idler, more interested in fooling than in delivering ("'livering"). We happened to have a round which went up to the limits of Mirfield northwards, in the direction of Roberttown and Liversedge. A Saturday came when we were still out in the afternoon as it had snowed, delaying still further our usual dilatoriness. I had not liked the slow progress and late finish, but the other boy had a stronger personality than mine. On that Saturday a customer gave us a letter to take back to Mr Rogers. He read it and told us that our late delivery had caused annoyance, adding his wrath to the customer's. I was angry and, in the evening, when my father had gone out, I fell to crying and said to my mother that I would not go to Rogers' shop again.

However, I soon moved on to Jeffrey's shop, again for 6d. There we used to have our pile made up by the ladylike Miss Jeffrey, who spoke kindly to us in the same tone as that which she used for serving customers.

Temptation to leave came when there was an opening at North's shop at 9d and I went there. Miss North helped her old father in the sorting in a low room under the shop. They had a cart in a shed. We disturbed a family of mice once and Mr North rushed in stamping madly. We could catch a glimpse of what was on front pages sometimes. On one occasion a weekly had something about stars and I aired my knowledge about Sirius and Orion to Miss North. She found a moment to acknowledge it and with a smile to add a detail.

My Yorkshire Folk in the Early 1900s

On one round I had to walk through Bruce's blanket mill, near Battyeford Station. I had to go through the weaving shed to reach the manager's office, isolated from the noise but with glass windows allowing for a view into the shed. Everything in the shed was smothered in fluff, including the weavers, and the greasy floor was lumpy and black with the trodden dirt of years. Going down the stairs required care. The workers carried away with them the characteristic smell of oily mustiness even into their own homes. I noticed it impregnated on the clothes of the women who came to the Co-op. The smell struck me also as I entered the house of Jack Wright, my first violin teacher, as I approached him on Friday nights. My mother brought a trace of it with her into our house after her long day at the loom. But there was little fluff at Learoyd's where worsted, the finest kind of cloth, was woven, and she had had a walk of nearly two miles after getting off the tram. My father had a stronger smell about him with the oily mud caked on his boots and to some extent on his fustian trousers from walking along the passages of the mine.

In a field adjacent to the blanket mill long lengths of blankets used to be stretched out on lines and hooks. As I saw them in the sunshine there was perhaps a bleaching effect intended, as well as a sweetening of the smell. It may be that the expression 'on tenter hooks' is derived from that stretching out.

On my paper round I had to call at the old Three Nuns Inn, at the entrance to the cart road leading to my father's pit. The Inn had an inner 'snug' for gentry and a simpler room for workmen. This had a bench along the wall side, a

few hard chairs nearer the coal fire for winter and a flagged floor strewn with sand for ease of sweeping, as not much use was made of the scraper at the side of the door. There was a spittoon at each side of the hearth to facilitate the accuracy of the saliva with the alternate sucking and spitting while smoking pipes. Many of the men I met in there, teamers mostly at that time of the morning, preferred the short clay pipe, retained sometimes till there was little left but the stump. They gradually changed colour from pure white to a deepening brown. Others had the full-length churchwarden variety, and a way of holding it with forefinger cocked over the stem giving an air of greater dignity. Navvy types of men used the stumpy pipe, often with the bowl whimsically inverted.

There was not the slightest attempt at soft comfort, but then the working men who called in for their pints had very little of that at home either. Anything like 'soft furnishings' would have been unsuitable, because all who entered wore rough dirty clothes.

My father made a grate, ie the frame of bars, for the fireplace at that inn. This came about because of the link between the inn and The Three Nuns Pit up the cart road behind it, where my father was blacksmith. That fireplace which my father was ordered to make was an acknowledgement of the good service provided by the publican. When anyone important came to the pit, dinner was ordered for the officials and the managers. It was brought up from the inn to the office.   My father used to describe the difference between these meals and his teacake.

Like the miners he carried his meal to work in a handkerchief. The miners had their handkerchiefs slung on the belt at the rear, on which was also a can containing tea, as the meal would have to be underground. They carried nothing to the workface in their hands, which had to be as free as possible for holding on during the drop down from the pit shaft in the cage, which was open-ended for running the corves in. Hands needed to be as free as possible also for riding on the trams at the bottom. Nevertheless, they had to manage always to take the safety lamp with them.

I went down to the yard in front of the Three Nuns Inn sometimes in summer after Sunday School and church in the afternoon along with boys who were going to hold horses. I tried this activity but lacked the cheerful cheek necessary to get a penny from visitors coming out after breaking their waggonette outing for a pint.

One day I saw there an act of some courage. At that time, in fact for a long time, there were navvies working in our neighbourhood on the railway cutting with its embankment and the construction of the Huddersfield Sewage Works at Cooper Bridge. This was ruinous to the amenities of the Three Nuns area, the air being filled with flies, necessitating covering one's face with a handkerchief for a distance of a quarter of a mile. Two navvies got into a fight outside the inn. The Mirfield police sergeant, not in uniform but in Sunday clothes with umbrella, was in the vicinity. He went to the two men, grabbed one with each hand, allowed his umbrella to drop on the ground, ignoring it while he walked the two men, both considerably bigger than him, along the Wakefield Road. From the place of arrest to the Police Station would be more than a mile. Spectators watched. We did not hear a word said.

On my newspaper round I called at two other public houses above the Three Nuns Inn, up the road leading from Huddersfield to Leeds: The Pear Tree and The Horseshoe. They failed to survive, being too near to the Three Nuns which was at the junction with the main road down the Calder valley. Up Mirfield Moor, I called at another inn, The White Gate. It had a white gate suspended from the wall above the entrance, on which was inscribed:

This gate hangs high
And hinders none
Refresh and pay
And travel on.

Almost opposite, on the side road, I called at Roehead, a big house in extensive grounds and

Roe Head, where Charlotte Brontë was pupil and teacher, near the boundary with Hartshead. With nearby Robin Hood Inn, the limit of my newspaper round.

(Joe's charcoal sketch shows the extension to the right.)
a good view towards the Pennines. This was where Charlotte Brontë had been pupil and teacher. Her father would know about , for his one-time parish of Hartshead was near. Charlotte said she found it irksome to try to get some instruction into local dullheads. The house has now been taken over by Verona Fathers as a seminary for Catholic boys intending to go into the missionary field.

I visited good houses and slums. Not far from Roehead, a door would open and the stench issuing took my breath away. There were ragged clothes piled up against the wall, and the woman herself was a bundle of the same sort. Why she wanted a newspaper, I could not understand. She kept me waiting too long with arguments about how much she owed.

Alongside the canal at Battyeford were some industrial premises at which the work was to extract oil from extremely greasy sacks which arrived in loads. I had to walk past to a house where I delivered a newspaper. The smell was nauseating. Above our house at Kitson Hill was a neighbour who worked there as a cooper concerned with the repair of barrels into which the oil was collected. An employee at that mill was subject to fits. As I passed one Saturday morning he fell down in the road at the side of the water. One of the workmen nearby, annoyed at this troublesome interruption, shouted "Chuck 'im i't cut!". I watched to see whether this advice would be taken but the other men just lifted the unconscious man on one side and went on with their work.

This falling down in fits was not new to me. We had a classmate at the Nab School who toppled off the bench at times with flickering eyelids and frothing mouth. He was a big, sturdy lad, enjoying immunity from rough treatment as we were always afraid of being accused of bringing on one of his attacks. He used to be dragged out into the porch and left to lie there and await recovery.

Such early experiences were useful to me long afterwards when I watched a boy in one of my classes at Carlton School gradually going over to sink on to the floor, and again, even long after that, when a girl at St Martin's at Brighouse went down. The change in the times was shown in this matter from the annoyance of "Chuck 'im i't cut!" and the dragging out to the solicitude of the 1950s. Then mats were brought and blankets, with a telephone call and a nurse arriving with the ambulance for the patient to be taken home for rest and a holiday.

The three newspaper shops for whom I worked gave me in all a wide range of travel in our village, which was known amongst us as the largest Village in the largest Riding in the largest County in England. On the south I ranged as far as Upper Hopton across the river, to the boundary with Liversedge (later part of Spenborough) on the north, and my cart went with me.

The main part of my stock consisted of *The Dewsbury Reporter* and *The Dewsbury and District News*. Remarkably such a small town could produce two weekly newspapers. They had sections for all the little suburbs and rural areas. Minute trivialities were collected. I spent little time looking at these, as we got *The Dewsbury Reporter* at home. I looked forward to the pleasure of pausing before delivering *Comic Cuts* to keep abreast of the exploits of Weary Willie and Tired Tim. Another paper of the same sort, *Chips*, also delayed my progress. The most thrilling of all, *The Police Budget*, always had a picture on the front depicting the most gruesome moment of a recent atrocity.

I took care, when pausing to rest on my cart and look at these things for a short time (though sometimes I had an uneasy feeling that the time had not been short enough), to keep out of sight of the house where I ought to have delivered. There was a big house standing in spacious grounds at the junction of Coppin Hall Lane and Church Lane, where the gentleman, Mr Humphreys, was angry at late delivery, and like the drawing inspector at my school, called me a "young monkey".

A kindly woman customer down Lea Green used to give me a teacake, white and hard, which I ate avidly, having a good appetite after the early morning start, but I had indigestion sometimes.

At Christmas we newspaper lads could look forward to a few Christmas Boxes, and I have gone home with two or three shillings. I was determined to spend some of this as I liked and bought a flash lamp, a thing of magic to us. Having bought it, I realised that I dared not take it home, so I buried it in a lane in a heap of clinkers. It had gone when I had later to go to retrieve it.

At home the Christmas custom of hanging up a stocking was observed for a few years when I was a boy. Over our fireplace we had a broad stone along which ran a string with a peg dangling in the middle. This peg could be propped against the stone to make the string stand out. Clothes that were hung here dried more quickly than those on the strings fastened on beams running along the ceiling. (On one beam, by the way, at a place nearest to the door was a stout hook for hanging a flitch of bacon, but not used for that in our time.) Before going to bed on Christmas Eve I fastened a stocking on the string with a safety-pin. Next morning it contained a new penny in the toe, an orange, nuts (mainly monkey nuts), some barcelonas (hazel nuts) and two or three lima nuts, all surmounted by a well polished apple.

The only other personal gift I ever received at home was on the day I was five. My mother baked for me a teacake containing many more currants than was usual for my father's dinner teacake, and I had permission to eat it just when I liked, which was, of course, while it was still warm.

My employment as a seller of newspapers came to an end with the scholarship to the Grammar School and, by a curious coincidence, I left my round to Tom Wood who three years earlier had initiated me. He was glad to get the ninepence. The time taken to earn this 'paper money' was six or seven hours. The experience was useful and helped me to broaden my acquaintance with boys and, to a little extent, with the world of work.

I considered other attempts to earn money. I went down sometimes in the summer holidays to the graveyard at Christ Church and talked to the verger *cum* grave-digger, Alan Hepworth, labouring below. I went to watch him. He said: "Come down and have a go". I tried my hand at the work; it was dirty and hard, much of the excavation having to be through stone, using chisel and maul. There were times of worry about not having a grave ready for a funeral, and Alan's patience was tried by the vicar who would come along from his vestry and require a message to be taken.

Alan was not a very strong man, and Nathan Clarkson, a miner, used to call in at the graveyard to help on his way home in the afternoon. Nathan had married the sister of the mother of Harry Senior who sat near me at the Nab School and gave me a ration of hen corn to chew in class, and with whom I played music in the evening. Nathan, like most other manual workers, did not hurry home, or anywhere else. Big and ponderous, he had nothing else to do on returning home but to eat a slow, enormous meal and then saunter across the road to the Nab Working Men's Club and sit with a pipe over beer till closing and bedtime.

Alan Hepworth had been a neighbour at the back of our house. One day I saw him come up the hill, turn the corner round our coalplace and go round the back. He reappeared carrying a box under his arm, about suitable for a big doll. I was curious about this and, when I was down in the churchyard watching him making a grave, asked about his visit. The box had contained a stillborn baby. Alan pointed to the bottom edge of the graveyard and said he had not kept count of the number of such internments he had carried out under that wall. The wall separated the church land from the meadow beyond. Running along the bottom of the burial ground, to about six feet away from the wall, there was waste land separated from the consecrated ground by a wide path. The little boxes had to be buried and merely covered with earth in unconsecrated ground.

We never heard of any woman going to hospital for the confinement or receiving any attention except at the birth, and that out of neighbourly kindness by women friends. The verger's off-hand observation to me reflected the consequence not unlikely to happen. The remark came home to me as my cousin Minnie, daughter of my father's oldest sister, had died in that way.

The woman who had lost the child also lost her husband. Her first name was May and she continued to live alone as our neighbour round the back. But this solitude ceased to be a matter of choice, and it became evident that she was prospecting for a second husband. Various interested parties came on the scene and, to our about 50% annoyance, May chose to conduct her conversational experiments at the corner of our coalplace, with much jolly talk and hilarious outbursts till after we had gone to bed, tantalised between the desire to get to sleep and the frustration of catching only half sentences in the merry interviews. May made her choice and settled down to quiet docility.

My Yorkshire Folk in the Early 1900s

On Fridays I carried a supply of eggs from Old Gray's farm to a mansion next to the Armoury drill hall used by the Territorials. I had a glimpse into what had been usual in such houses before the First World War. There was a huge stone-floored kitchen with massive ovens. Suspended on the walls above was an array of cooking utensils of shining copper and brass. High up was a row of bells with wide-open springs so that when a rope hanging by the fireside in any particular room above was pulled the bell began to swing on its spring. An indicator above showed an oscillating disc in a connected glass case, and told which one of the maids had to hurry along in response. They wore white pinafores. In all, I had a two-mile journey to the mansion, but I got a penny.

Old Gray's little farm was at the bottom of our hill and in the school holidays I strolled down there to look into the farmyard. If 'Owd Gray' was doing anything there I ventured in, timidly at first, to watch him. I think he did not know who I was, for he never made any contact with his neighbours, his whole life being concentrated, to his satisfaction, on the work of his little farm. He made no objection to my presence.

Under the shed he had a large tub for the kitchen leftovers which he collected from the College of the Resurrection opposite his fields.. He also went to Fieldhead across the road. For these journeys he had a pony and a flat cart. I went with him to take the Fieldhead laundry to a house in Mirfield Moor. The roads were quiet enough for me to hold the reins when the going was straight. I watched him filling the bucket with the swill to take to the trough. On one occasion he scooped up a rat from the tub. He had apparently not noticed it, so I drew his attention to it. He said it was alright: the pigs would eat it with the rest. On one occasion when his son was free from his work at the currier's shop at the top of the hill, we could hear, from a hundred yards away, a terrified squealing. Rings were being thrust through the noses of young pigs, so that when roaming in the field they would not disturb the turf too much.

At Old Gray's farm the barn was contiguous with the house. The smell of the hay was very pleasant. Pigeons had access. I don't think he fed them: they could look after themselves in the fields and with what was thrown down for the hens. They were also a cheap form of food. I watched how he killed a pigeon by putting its head between finger and thumb and pressing the skull in.

An occasional bit of extra work in the evening in good weather was a pleasant change. Haymaking got a few of the men outside. During haymaking time I went to help with the gathering of the hay, receiving it for stowing as Old Gray lifted it up onto the fork. I was doing that when I was not strong enough to have lifted a forkful myself. There seems to have been some concern about the stack sweating. A long iron rod was thrust in and left for a while, then pulled out to be felt.

Old Gray grew no corn, but there was such a field near our Elementary School, and during the whole of one day there was a throbbing sound. A huge traction engine, of the same size as the steam rollers used for bedding-in the dross in road repairs, had come into the field. It was also exactly like the engines used for producing electric current at fairgrounds. It was pulling a massive threshing machine, which turned out separately the bundles of straw and the flow of grain. A crew of several men was kept busy. The invention of the use of steam had long since made a great improvement on the use of the flail, but was much inferior to the combine harvester.

There was haymaking on a larger scale in the fields of the Fieldhead estate, entered only twenty yards above our house. Once the grass had been cut, with an optimistic guess about the likelihood of a few days of fine weather, several men joined the farmer for the haymaking. A few of us lads went into the fields for a chance of raking the hay into the swatches. We were allowed to mount the carts for stowing, easier than the forking for us. At noon we went down across the meadows to the farm for 't'lahnce' (the allowance), fat sandwiches and a stone jar of beer. The best part was riding on top of the hay back to the farm.

Old Gray had two large gardens, for one of which I helped collect leaves in autumn, fallen from the trees of the Fieldhead wood across the road. No Local Authority workmen went round cleaning the roads in our neighbourhood. With the leaves a large bed was made for rotting and later digging into the soil. Flowers and fruit grew in the other garden on the other side of the house. At Harvest Festival time, children came to buy flowers for decorating the church. I was given a bunch.

The leaves lying thickly across the causeway and the gutter caused me to have a mishap. A woman up the hill had asked me to wheel the baby out in the pram, which I did down the hill on the causeway. There was such a thick covering of leaves that I misjudged the edge and tipped the baby into the road, where fortunately there were enough leaves to act as shock absorbers. Of course, I did not report the mishap.

Pheasants appeared in the wood at Fieldhead, and the young men working on the upper floor of the currier's shop noticed them. They went over the wall and set traps. I did not hear of any success. Their intrusion into the wood was made less risky by the distance from the farm, as was ours at the approach of bonfire time.

Another poacher had better luck with pheasants. Sir George Armytage's Kirklees Estate adjoined the Three Nuns Pit. One afternoon, when the steward was out shooting, a miner went over the wall into the wood and had the luck to see a pheasant drop into the thick undergrowth. The steward had seen the direction of the fall and came out of the field into the wood. But the alert intruder had already got the bird nicely concealed. The steward entered the wood. Not being able to avoid detection, the miner lowered his trousers before being seen. The steward approached and asked if he had seen a pheasant. The man said "No" and was embarrassed at being caught in that predicament (excusable in view of the poor sanitary facilities at the pit) and the steward felt the same also and withdrew.

11

Games and Entertainments

We boys nearly always played with our own lot when not at school. Going down once in the evening, to the 'low road' (the main road leading through Mirfield from Huddersfield to Dewsbury) to see how the boys played in that locality, we found that, even at that short distance, we were regarded as 'off-comers'. On Kitson Hill I played with the Copleys, the Holmeses, and two Fernley boys from further up the road who went to Knowl Council School. This difference made for a polite acquaintanceship, in contrast with the unconcerned intimacy with the boys living almost on our doorstep, and who were with me at Battyeford National School.

Knowing the Fearnley boys had its advantage, as in the summer I could go their way and roam in the hayfield and jump about with them on the stack in the barn. In the hen pen there was a goat with which we skirmished, risking tupping.

In the schoolyard there were two games in particular. In our kind of leap-frog, two teams were picked after the preliminary 'footing' by the captains. 'Footing' meant that two boys stood about three yards apart and approached each other, putting heel to toe until one boy's boot overlapped the other's toes. The team chosen, the front boy supported himself against the wall, his mates getting behind him with heads down, and each gripping the hips of the boy in front of him. The remaining boys in the yard gathered behind in a bunch to run, one at team A the next at team B, and leapt on to the back of the 'caterpillar'. So we piled up, clinging desperately till one team collapsed under the strain and the weight.

The commonest pastime was marbles, of which I kept a precious supply in a bag at home, with a small number in my pocket for use as daily working capital. There were little acts of generosity in this game. In order to get back into play a boy who had lost all would be set up again with the gift of a few plain ones. The variegated glass marbles were the more valuable ones and were used as a target for the plain ones made usually of painted baked clay.

There were two main forms of the marbles game. On the large flag at the entrance to the school porch a glass alley was put at one edge and the attackers had to flick a marble with the thumb from a bend in the forefinger, the intention being to win the alley by hitting it, the owner meanwhile appropriating the wide shots. That was the form of the game we indulged in when our class had the good fortune to get a period of extra play for having had the best attendance during the previous week. We could be sure of not having our play disturbed by other boys rushing in and out of the porch.

Another, slower, form was to scratch a ring in the ground, someone staking some marbles in it for attack from a line at a certain distance. It was a kind of simple snooker. As for the name of these games, if a teacher had asked us what we were doing, we should have said that we were playing at marbles, but amongst ourselves we were "laikin' at taws".

Our boyhood pastimes, involving things which could be carried in the pockets, had in common an appeal to our acquisitive instinct. As I look back, it occurs to me as remarkable that, keen as we were to accumulate things, no one thought of gratifying this instinct in the way which could have been the most profitable, ie by money stakes. Perhaps the dearth of money preserved our innocence. Had playing for halfpennies been indulged in, snobbery would have followed; instead of participation by all, there would have been pauper spectators. Again, the good example of parents helped. When, after my father's retirement, he and my mother were drawn into a sweepstake during a coaching tour, I was shocked at this hitherto unheard-of lapse.

'Football cards' was a fashionable game during my time at the Nab School. It is claimed that these were originated by a Bradford man, John Baines, at the beginning of the century. They were sold in halfpenny packets, and had shield shaped portraits of sports stars. Like marbles they varied in value, the ones with golden rims being more esteemed than the plain ones. The game was to put a card against the wall and let it fall. If it over-lapped a card already down, even to the slightest extent, both cards were picked up by the winner. It was necessary for someone to drop first. This boy was picked, as in our other games, by footing.

Attempts at football were made, but we had little room (there were no parks or public recreation grounds in Mirfield) and never a proper ball. We tried to invent one by tying rags round a small block of wood, a clumsy thing but it lasted for a short time and was not in danger of rising to break any windows. There was a larger kind of ball to kick if one of us was lucky enough to get a bladder at the butcher's on slaughtering day. One could be had for ½d. The neck of the bladder was greasy but we could inflate it by vigorous blowing with the stem of a clay pipe and tying with string. A game with a bladder was an erratic activity as it jumped and bounced in all directions. It never lasted long; it dried and became brittle.

Mention of string reminds me that when I was quite young the verger at church, Mr Brewer, requiring string for something he was helping us with, found that not one of us had any. He was contemptuous about this and said we should always carry on us a penknife and some string. I took this seriously and acquired a penknife as soon as could. I have carried a knife ever since and am only at my present age overcoming the habit of hoarding string in a pocket. The only time when my penknife was not in my pocket was during my active service in the Navy, when I carried a jack-knife on a lanyard looped round my waist, ready at a moment's notice to cut away ropes which were securing means for floating. My name was on a little brass plate fixed to the knife. It was a necessary part of my equipment.

My Yorkshire Folk in the Early 1900s

Cricket came up with the right season. An hour or two of leisure could be spent from time to time watching an open-air game. Steady, safe games were those of the Resurrection students' matches. The Primitive Methodist Cricket Club played cricket down at Fox Royd, and in the right weather one could loiter on the path at the side of the field and watch the valiant, often ludicrous, efforts of unshapely and untrained local lads. Christ Church also had a cricket field, and there was the same excitement of anticipation of a lucky boundary or a disgraceful flying stump, either result following from the same sort of mighty swipe. The remarks of jeering friends at the shamefaced, retiring batsman were part of the fun. The Vicar came along sometimes for a few minutes, but he remained apart from the little crowd and waited for the most respectable of the men spectators to come up and listen to his observations of patronising approval.

I played cricket with the Holmeses 'on t'yard', the space between our square block of four houses and the currier's shop, wide enough to admit horse and waggon to the shed when a load of leather or skeps came and interrupted us. We also played cricket out in the road, there being little traffic to cause us to stand aside. Indeed I have seen a dog asleep in the middle of the road. My father once joined us in cricket, taking the bat and maliciously sending the ball as far as he could down the hill for me to run after, and he did not earn his innings as we had to by fielding. I once won a bat in the sports held on a Saturday afternoon in summer. These were a kind of general sports for children, arranged by the schools. The bat was too weak for our use and lost its handle, but I did some home woodwork and made a strong one-piece one which did not have the disadvantage of a spliced handle. Possession of something necessary for a game improved one's standing with the group. The Holmeses supplied the wickets, pegged into a piece of wood for a base and not requiring to be driven into the ground. The expression "He's takken 'is bat home" meant that a boy had ceased to play with the others, at whatever the game happened to be, and gone home in a bad temper.

We played hop-scotch a little on the causeway flags, but this was regarded as more suitable for girls, and still is. Tops came into season in about February. First I had a fat top, driven with a whip, and later a more slender top which spun after being flung down when a long piece of string had been carefully wound round. I acquired a little kite, too, and got much interest out of fitting a suitable tail. I also tried to make a bigger kite with brown paper, flour, paste and split cane. A boy with more spending money had a box kite and a huge roll of string. The field beyond the currier's shop was at the top of a steep hill and in a good wind there were very high flights achieved.

Arrow-throwing came in, and the cutting, feathering and throwing practice occupied some time pleasantly in the summer holiday. A craze developed for slinging. A strip of leather had a hole cut near each end and strings attached. A stone having been placed on the leather, the sling was swung vigorously round, one string being then released. The winner of the game was the one whose stone went furthest. Once I was foolishly practising in the road outside our house. There was no-one about. My stone went through a small pane of a low-decker up the road.

Apparently the incident went unnoticed. The inhabitants must have been out. I was unhappy about this. If I had been found out, I should have had my father to face and the problem of paying. I was not found out, but had my punishment in the twinge of conscience I felt whenever I went up the hill.

One Saturday evening in summer a drunken man was wending his to-left-to-right way along Kitson Hill where some of us were playing, and laughter and jeering broke out amongst us. One boy threw a big atone in the direction of the man, who tried to curse out his annoyance, but was incapable of changing course to get near enough to us. During the following week I had been to Farrers' farm for the usual extra quart of milk for the baking, when I saw this man approaching. I was so alarmed at the possibility of retribution that I turned aside and jumped down into the field on the left, a drop of about three yards. Fortunately I spilt little of the milk. When I had crept along to where I could get back up on to the road, the man was far away. I had probably underestimated the effect of alcohol on the memory.

Another game, definitely mischievous, played on selected victims on dark winter nights, was window-tapping. A weight of some kind was fastened to the end of a piece of string long enough to reach to a place of hiding. The string was passed through a staple which could be stuck into the wooden frame of the upper window. The weight was pulled up and down to make a scraping, rattling noise on the window pane. As soon as someone opened the door to seek the cause of the trouble, the weight and the staple were jerked away and hauled in rapidly, leaving us with the problem of whether to lie still where we were or to try to sneak away rapidly and silently.

That was for dark evenings, as was also the sham parcel, neatly tied up and containing dry horse manure, always available on the road. We placed the small parcel against the wall at the side of the flags of the causeway near enough to a gas lamp to be seen. It might be thought to have dropped out of someone's bag. We waited to see the reaction of passers-by. We had achieved success when curiosity could not be resisted and the parcel was opened.

On winter evenings we few boys on our hill played hide-and-seek, easy enough as a few yards from the gas lamp all nooks and corners were black. When obscurity made the search too difficult, derisive and provocative cries stimulated the seekers.

It is evident that some of our play, including mischief, depended on darkness. There were gas lamps along the causeway on the far side of the road, long before a gas pipe was laid up our side. Each lamp required individual attention twice a day, as darkness fell and as daylight returned. The lamp-lighter made his round twice, each time with a pole surmounted by a cylindrical oil container for maintaining a flame. There was apparently no wick, for there was always some smoke issuing. There was a lever at the bottom of the glass frame, which was pushed to admit gas, before raising the pole higher to kindle the flame. In the morning, there was need only to push the lever. The length of the journeys on foot caused wide intervals between the lightings and the extinguishings.

The method I have described was in advance of that which I saw after I left Mirfield. I saw a man lighting lamps at the side of the Town Hall in Bradford. He mounted a ladder with a box of matches to open a window of the frame. Lighting must have tried his patience in windy weather. The visits to the lamp posts were interesting to watch. The first time our son Brian, as a very young boy, expressed a choice of career, it was that of a lamp-lighter.

There was an organised afternoon sport on one Saturday called 'Hare and Hounds', played by youths in their late teens. Two of them set off carrying a bag slung over a shoulder and containing a supply of ribbon-like paper edgings. They were the Hares, and ran across fields and jumped over walls, dropping paper at intervals to indicate a course not known to the Hounds, and perhaps not to the Hares themselves in advance. We youngsters watched with interest and decided to take part. The Hares had to be given plenty of time to disappear from view. That was our opportunity to run in and gather paper to lay a divergence leading to nothing. Our fun of course was to hide and observe the bewilderment which ensued.

Running with a hoop was a permanently casual game. It could be indulged in individually while doing an errand, or it could be competitive. My father made me a strong, perfectly round iron hoop of about 1 foot 6 inches in diameter, with iron driver to match. This iron rod had a hook at one end and a loop for gripping at the other. None of my playmates had so good a hoop. We lived in a good place for running with a hoop. Down Kitson Hill the hoop ran fast by itself and I ran behind, retarding with the hook and putting the driver now to one side now to the other to steer. On the level the hoop had to be propelled with the hook. To propel and steer at the same time was difficult. Little races were an exciting form of competition and could be indulged in any time as we had the empty road to ourselves.

Girls had hoops also but these were much larger and lightly constructed of overlapping strips of bent wood. They were driven by being beaten with a stick. It required practice to drive in a steady direction. Hoop races for girls were a usual item in sports programmes, collisions and collapses adding to the fun of partisan supporters.

In their yard at our school, we could watch the girls play hop-scotch, jumping across squares scratched into the earth. Skipping was popular with the girls, either individually to attempt the highest number without trapping the rope, or with two girls holding the rope which a queue of girls ran into in turn. Singing sometimes accompanied the turns. Most of the time, however, was spent in forming groups to gossip.

Older girls on summer evenings did not go straight home after church or chapel, but went to stroll along the causeway of 'Park Bottom', along the wall side of Blake Park, an open area between Mirfield and Ravensthorpe. There two or three girls, linked together, encountered two or three youths strolling in the opposite direction. Smiles and compliments to the weather led to slowing down at the next encounter and awkward attempts to find something further to say. It was a beginning and could lead to 'walking out' on the quiet before letting parents know that a more serious development was taking place. Social relationships did not usually extend beyond the locality, so that when the courting became regular and open, both of the couple were known and social approval followed

My Yorkshire Folk in the Early 1900s

Knur and Spell was a well-known game for working men. There was a see-saw arrangement for placing the knur, and the spell consisted of a long, pliable cane having on its end a wooden shape like half a bottle split lengthways. The tee was tipped with a gentle tap from the end of the spell and the knur given a violent blow as it began to fall after its little jump into the air. Contests and bets stimulated skill and interest.

We boys had our own simplified form of Knur and Spell, using a knur made from a piece of wood sharpened at each end, and any convenient stick for the spell. A blow on the pointed end of the knur made it rise from the ground, and skill was shown in being able to hit the knur at all. The distances achieved were much less than those by the men. For scoring, comparative lengths of shots were measured by striding.

Any leisure after I returned home at eight years of age from the Copleys', when they left the hill, tended to become more solitary as time went on. The few boys of my age in our immediate neighbourhood went to work as soon as their age allowed, while at the same time my time at home increased. The summer holiday at the Grammar School lasted seven weeks, and we did not go away for holidays. In this respect we differed little from others on the hill.

Amongst the children there was little to do with animals. I cannot recall any boy or girl having a pet dog or bird, except a boy in my class who kept rabbits. The idea of acquiring one so pleased me that I went home with him and, having visited his hutch, said I would give him sixpence for one. Fortunately his mother stepped in to ask how I would keep it. I had no box or anything else. My idea was to let it live in the coalplace. It was lucky for me that there was no sale, for I should have got into trouble at home.

Interests for working men were whippet racing after rabbits, and pigeon breeding and racing. A man living a few doors above us was a keen pigeon breeder; he used to spend hours sitting in his cote with his pigeons, with no apparent desire to do anything else. They were a consolation, for we discovered that he had condemned himself to bachelorhood by fathering an illegitimate child. When my father got an aerial for his wireless from the chimney to a high pole at the end of the garden at the back, the pigeon fancier complained to the authorities, and corks had to be put on the aerial as well as on the telephone wires in the vicinity.

More respectably for the men, bowls were played at Working Men's Clubs. In the case of the nearby Nab Workingmen's Club, the construction of a bowling green was an improvement, getting the men out of the smoky room, developing a little pride in skill and providing an impersonal topic for talk. Interclub bowling competitions had a broadening influence. Our local weekly newspapers stimulated this interest with publication of results and names. With the new interest the beer moved also. Some men changed places as competitors on the green below or as pint-sipping spectators on the verandah.

Gentlemen played golf on ground far away at the top of Hopton on the other side of the Calder. Indication of status by getting to the golf course by motorcar was beginning only at the latter part of my time at Mirfield. Ladies (and some gentlemen) played tennis.

There were football teams, rising suddenly into vigour and disappearing as fast, composed of lads in their teens. Rough crowds gathered to watch these matches. The spectators often had a bad effect, with their crude cries instigating vengeance. Fights were always probable. The prestige of a player who put up his fists, challenging, soared high. Our mild-tempered, middle-aged verger *cum* grave-digger unwisely yielded to a request to be referee. One Saturday he paid for a verdict with a black eye.

My father never took any part in out-of-the-house activities. He had seen something of football as a lad at Low Moor, but in my time at home he would not even cross the road to watch the Resurrection students play their clean, enthusiastic game, and to me expressed his contempt for the 'flannelled fools'.

The interest he developed after his retirement showed the change in his sociability and the need for something to fill the vacuum left by release from work. When he got wireless, my father grew keen about Saturday teatime football results. He even went to see a semi-final match between Huddersfield and Arsenal, and got a fright. Aloft and fat he was in danger of being crushed in the surging mob of 67,000, besides having little opportunity to follow the game. That was his only attempt to get first-hand experience of high-standard play. By a coincidence, it was the same for me. I had travelled from Shelf to see that match.

Expeditions

One Saturday afternoon in summer our curate, J E Roberts, arranged to take a party of men and women to Kirklees Park. My father

Joseph H Hird

knew Sir George Armytage's steward, who, like other people passing the workshop in the pit-yard, would loiter and peep in and get into a brief conversation with the men at work. Through this contact, my father got permission from Mr Alcock, the steward, to join the visiting party, and we went to Kirklees. There were not many things to see, but we did get an idea of a gentleman's amenities: an extensive estate, containing deer, pheasants, woods, shooting-lodge, large garden enclosed in high walls and with long greenhouses containing vines. We went to a railed-in grave on the hillside and Mr Alcock read the inscription commemorating the burial there of Robin Hood on the site where he had shot his last arrow to mark the place for Little John.

J E Roberts, as another of his enterprises, once organised a church outing to Crow Nest Park at Dewsbury. The destination was only three miles away, but the trip lasted from early on Saturday afternoon till well on into the evening. There were weeks of arranging about it, with ticket-printing, name and money taking at the services in church on Sunday afternoons. A tea was arranged at the house which is now the museum in the park and we sat on the grass out-side to eat our packed food. Though so near, many of the children had never seen this park. Crow Nest Park was familiar to our family for my father liked to go there, walking over the fields, on Sunday evenings in summer to hear the bands playing. For this purpose also he liked Greenhead Park at Huddersfield, where there were fine military bands in their brilliant uniforms. I remember a favourite piece was Tchaikovsky's *1812 Overture.*

My Yorkshire Folk in the Early 1900s

Short journeys of a few miles to one of the neighbouring towns, which seemed further away then when all or most of the travel was on foot, showed something in my father's temperament. For the rest of the week he had only work and house, and a craving for crowds came over him by way of reaction. Sometimes he took me, and so I became familiar with Heckmondwike, Dewsbury and Huddersfield.

To reach Huddersfield we walked two miles and then had a twopenny tram-ride. In the basement of the market in Huddersfield was a stall where sarsaparilla was on sale at a penny a glass. The man topped it up with another liquid giving it a delicious piquant taste. My father also bought chlorodyne tablets, of which he continued to carry a supply in a pocket of his going-out suit to the end of his life.

Halifax we reached more rarely, and then with a second-hand clothes aim. Heckmondwike had a small market place where we indulged in trip to a stall.

Dewsbury had a large open-air market where, at a stall illuminated by hissing suspended lamps, we could have a small pork pie with peas, served on a plate and consumed under the eye of the stallholder. We could then move across the market place to where there were sales of lost, or cheap, objects. An auctioneer stood on a waggon, shouting continuously the cheapness and reliability of his offerings. He sold umbrellas and had the knack, while talking, of opening the umbrella and swinging his arm around to reverse it, and back again, presumably to show its firm structure. It was rarely my father succumbed to such sales talk, but one night he bought an umbrella when the bidding halted at half-a-crown, a strange purchase for him to make, for he despised the use of umbrellas. After that, though, he went out with it on a few Sunday evenings when it was fine, and he would not have to risk disturbing the neat, tight folds. It was never raised; he regarded an umbrella as evidence of elegance.

Such treats took place at irregular intervals on journeys away from our village but there were in Mirfield itself little centres for the indulgence of the firmly established habit, fish and chips.

Within fairly easy walking distance there were wooden huts called "chip 'oils" with coal-heated fish and chip pans and a counter on which was fixed the lever for pushing the potatoes through the honeycomb framework. This then shed the long square shapes into a bowl under the counter. The huts were so small that all the preparation had to be done in the space between the counter and the chip-pan. This was the washing and peeling of the potatoes, the cleaning and cutting of the fish and the bathing of it in batter before dropping it with a hiss into the boiling fat along with a bucketful of chips. If the customer arrived when all the fish and chips in the net above the pan had been sold, the tedium of waiting was relieved by watching all that process. The orders were "One o' awther!" or "Two o' fish 'n two o' chips" or modestly "Aw'p'th o' awther". After seasoning the food with vinegar and salt from the sprinklers, one could either stand in front of the small space between the counter and the door and eat straight from the two papers, a blank one and a piece of newspaper, or one could eat outside or take the fish and chips home wrapped in more newspaper.

My Yorkshire Folk in the Early 1900s

Bradford and Leeds were too far and expensive, but after his 'ship came home', my father would come with a railway excursion ticket to Bradford to stroll amongst the market crowds and eat peas and a pie in one of the market alcoves before getting back home in good time. In his last years my father was able not only to indulge his urge to rub shoulders in a crowd, but to recall the time half a century earlier when he and his mate, Herbert Slater, used to walk down Manchester Road together on Saturday night, eat peas and a pie or tripe, and occasionally go to a theatre.

There was an annual excursion, the church trip, a free ticket to which we in the choir had earned. It was a long day's outing by special train from Mirfield to the east coast or the west. In this way I had seen Blackpool, Southport, Scarborough, and Bridlington before the war gave me free trips to even more distant places. I had also been on a trip from Brighouse with my father to Belle Vue, Manchester, from which we arrived back home in the early hours after a walk in the darkness from Brighouse Station.

There were expeditions at the right season to gather yarrow and figwort, yarrow being for colds and figwort for the blood. As with the rhubarb wine and ink-making which I will describe shortly, we went beyond moderation with herbs. Of yarrow there was a fine bed extending along the waggon road running up to Hartshead beside the wall of Kirklees Estate. At the time when the plant was in flower I had to go there, since there was no one or any building within a great distance, and gather, tie up, and come back with a great bundle under my arm as darkness fell. Then there was the task of washing and drying them on a flag. If one had a cold, the cure was to drink strong yarrow tea, unpleasant, and go to bed to sweat, which we did thoroughly. There was less figwort, a square-stemmed plant which was found along the banks of the Spen Beck at Ravensthorpe, a short distance before its confluence with the River Calder. The drink made from this herb was distasteful, with a copious addition of Spanish juice bought in sticks and mixed with water.

Nettles were another herb used, but my father brought these home himself in the red handkerchief in which he had carried his midday teacake. There was a tip near his workshop overgrown with grass and nettles. I had the job of sorting out nettles from grass and nipping off suitable leaves. They were boiled with oatmeal. Nettles were for a spring cleansing of the blood. For this, too, we had an occasional brew of camomile flowers.

Two of the women who worked at my mother's mill were worshippers at the Zion Baptist Chapel. They helped in a fund-raising event, a bazaar which was an occasion for selling books of recipes contributed by the members (who in that way got their names in print as having helped). My mother bought a copy of the book for the bazaar in 1907, but she never attempted to make use of the recipes. I kept the book (and, as I have referred to, unsuccessfully attempted a recipe on one occasion). After the recipes, there was a section on Remedies, including 'Comfrey Root for weakness' and 'A Substitute for Brandy'. After that there came a Miscellaneous section: Live Long; How to Whiten the Nails; Kisses; How to Make a Happy Home; When You are in Low Spirits; How to

Become Good-Looking; Hygienic Sausage; A Cure for Baldness. The book included wise sayings like "A hair on the head is worth two in the brush".

A propos of plant remedies, my father, at the time when his baldness was extending, was anxious to reverse the deterioration and happened to hear of hair restoration by means of Irish moss. The process was to procure a packet of the dried seaweed, stew it and apply the juice to the crown of the head. The product of the cooking was a kind of slime, with which my father thickly covered the area already bare as well as the borders likely in the near future to diminish. The treatment could only be used in the evening, but my father wished to be thorough, and having sat in his chair all evening while the moss dried on, he added a further amount of juice before fitting one of my mother's mop caps, under which the hoped for beneficial effects could continue during the night. Perseverance with Irish moss went unrewarded.

Economies

My father was not a teetotaller, and I believe it was his careful use of money which kept him away from a use of leisure in which it was understood that sociability and consumption of alcoholic beverages were concomitant.

A compromise was attempted with the purchase of a barrel of beer, which fitted nicely into a recess in our little cellar. A spigot replacing the bung enabled a drink to be withdrawn easily. But that means failed, for there was no convenient time for the heavy vehicle, like the coal carts, to come up our hill when we were in, and I doubt whether it was considered very profitable to deliver one barrel. The beer must have come a long way, for there were no breweries in our neighbourhood.

My father therefore attempted to make his own beverage. It was to be rhubarb wine, made in our big baking bowl. For the fermentation I went to The Airedale Heifer for a quart of wet yeast. After the period thought suitable, which was more or less guesswork for there were no printed instructions, my father proceeded with bottling for storage in the cellar. There must have been some error in the method, for after a while, at a quiet time in the evening a series of startling explosions began, followed by the clatter of glass falling back on to the stone floor from various parts of the ceiling and walls. So my father became teetotal by habit if not by inclination. He liked a change of taste to follow his Sunday dinner, so for many years I had to go to a house up the road, where they had a whole crate of lime-juice-and-soda delivered. I disliked this errand. There was no profit on the bottle for them and, by keeping me waiting a long time before answering the door, they showed that they did not wish to be disturbed, but my father made me continue to go.

My initiative to create a drink was limited to obtaining a stick of Spanish juice (liquorish) so as to break it up into bits and put into a bottle for shaking to dissolve into beverage.

But it occurred to my father to think of brandy as 'medicine'. I do not know why there should have been difficulty in obtaining a bottle, but one evening we took a long walk to a club where a workmate had made an arrangement that when he saw my father at a certain point in the distance, he would come out with a bottle under his coat. My father's brandy was his 'medicine' for the rest of his life. After his retirement my father had some tendency to pay visits to the cellar for sips of medicine.

After his death I poured out some remaining. (His cheroots I gave to my Uncle Herbert.)

Sometimes on our Saturday outing to Huddersfield we would come across a collier who would ask my father into a public-house for a pint. I waited on the causeway. My father did not stay in long. His uneasiness in the kind of sociability of a public house was a saving. The collier's generosity was for favours rendered or invited in the matter of extra care or priority with his sharpened picks.

Another attempted economy concerned my supply of ink. We anticipated that I should probably have some years of writing to do. To avoid having to buy ink, my father decided to make some. We got a red cabbage, and with it produced in our big baking bowl enough coloured water to have served for all the writing I was likely to do in the rest of my life. Perseverance with the semi legibility of the liquid at last yielded to a recognition that the cabbage had been wasted.

A more effective economy was the disused coal-note ledgers my father had been bringing from the pit. The reverse sides were blank, but there were some queer contiguities on the scraps of paper I used for notes. The cost of so many cartloads of coal became mixed up with pious exhortations and a preparatory translation into Latin or a memory test of a geological fault. The pious exhortations came from another source of paper. When at last our vicar Old Benny retired he had left a large quantity of sermon notes in a cupboard in the vestry. These were pulled out and dumped into a great pile on the floor. Trained to be always on the look-out to 'sam things up', I had the idea of using the parts of paper free from writing, so there was soon another dump at our house for sorting out what could be used. I still have music mended with sermon notes.

An activity for me was reading. The means for this were scarce. There was a cupboard of library books at Mirfield Grammar School, and the English mistress lent these out, but the supply was inadequate. The only other means of borrowing books was from the Battyeford branch of the Huddersfield Co-op. There was an old catalogue on the counter at the side of the shop least used, and a book could be asked for. On my next visit the following week, I asked if it had come. The manager went round to look among the three or four sent. I had to trouble him on several weeks before being successful. Nothing recent was available.

My most interesting attempts to get access to books took place in a large second-hand bookshop in Huddersfield, opposite the Parish Church. I walked there in the summer holidays and told the old man what sort of book I wanted. He gave me permission to go round the rooms and into the cellar where languages were stored. I used to worry about taking so long and spending so little, but the man was slow and patient, and sometimes in a state of controlled inebriation. I got a few bargains very cheaply, perhaps the best being a volume of the entire works of Shakespeare, price one shilling.

Concerts and Cinema

Huddersfield Co-op had some Saturday evening concerts with literary readings, eg from Dickens. It was a pity that my father did not show more inclination to go there.

Here may be mentioned the coming of the cinema to Mirfield. Up to that time (I think it would be about 1910) I had seen no projected pictures except by means of the magic lantern. Pictures thrown on to a screen by this means had been a useful adjunct to our Lenten mid-week devotional concert with service, where we had an illustrated, musical version of *Pilgrim's Progress.*

My Uncle Lewis had a magic lantern and showed us a few slides, dimly reflected on the wall of the pantry from a light kindled with an oil lamp. Developments in lighting for the magic lantern were acetylene and then, with the spread of electricity, the two carbon sticks almost touching, and fusing brilliantly across the gap. Both these improvements were unreliable, acetylene with the difficulty of accurate valve and water adjustment, and the electricity because of the splutter and frequent failure of the carbons.

Public film shows came to Mirfield at the Town Hall at performances held in winter after church time. The showing of the film itself was not ample enough to occupy the whole time and there were other items, with the normal gas lighting of the hall. There were solo singing efforts by young amateurs, hand-bell ringing, and musical tapping of glasses with different quantities of water in them. At one performance a lad I had known at the Elementary School, Harold Pollard, produced a tune by having a big circular frame round the circumference of which were revolving discs. He had something in his hand to touch the discs in order to produce, clumsily and slowly but recognisably, some well-known tune.

But we were impatient for the film. Three subjects I can remember: *Don't go down the mine, daddy* and *A little child shall lead them* about reconciliation between quarrelling husband and wife, and a film about the Boer War in which a British sentry was ambushed. The projector rattled a good deal and the acetylene lighting did not make a bright enough reflection. The alternation of picture and blackness on the screen, keeping time with the rattling, was tiring for the eyes, but the full hall of people enjoyed the thrilling novelty. Such shows we at first referred to as 'moving pictures'. then we said 'cinematograph' till, with frequent use, the word was shortened.

At about the time that the cinema was arriving, there rushed in the roller-skating craze. Near the Battyeford Station a corrugated-iron building was erected and had performances in the evening with a matinée on Saturdays. Harry Holmes, the hunchback boy neighbour of ours, was able to get a change from the family cobbling business by fitting and removing skates at the skating rink. The building was little more than a shed, almost without amenities. No skill worth watching was developed. The monotony of noisily pushing one way round the small area diminished the interest. The place adjusted itself to the changing fashion. To become a picture house it required little expense: a projector at one end, white sheet at the other, and fairly plain seats between. Below the middle of the screen the musician at the upright piano watched the trend of mood and interest in the story to bring down on to the stand an appropriate copy of music from the supply spread out on top.

Larger picture houses could support a trio, including violinist and cellist. Such players had moved from the theatre, and there were good amateurs doing two jobs, the day occupation being something quite different. The course of live musical performance in halls of passive entertainment ran thus: theatre orchestra, trios in cinemas, organist, out. For a time the largest cinemas could support a full orchestra, and then a clever organist in time for whistling or singing to, before becoming merely soothing sound covering the ice-cream interval.

A spotlight on the console reminded the audience that the music was coming to them live. Amplified, canned music drove out the solitary descendant of the theatre orchestra. The manager of one of the largest cinemas in Bradford, the Ritz, told me, when I referred to the length of time they had an organist, that he had been appointed to attract larger audiences. He had been kept on because some people were staying too long in the continuous performances. If there was a queue the manager interrupted the film at a convenient place and called upon the organist to play and stir the seat huggers.

12

The Three Nuns Pit

My father had pride in his skill as a blacksmith. His more specific work was in repairing the iron parts of the corves and sharpening picks, the latter of which in the heyday of the pit he had to do for over a hundred colliers. He also had to shoe the horse which from time to time made the journey from Low Moor, a job he disliked, as the big animal's leg was too heavy for him. In addition he made grates, hammers, and fire-irons. He was also involved with the wiring around the pit and, given training, he would have made an electrician.

Proof of this was his fitting up of an electric clock with wet battery in the bedroom of our house with a switch at the bed-head for my mother to stop the alarm. This was not a great success. She was always so short of sleep that it was found wiser to have to get out of bed. The chilly steps on a dark winter's morning to feel for the catch at the side of the clock on the mantelpiece about five yards away had a reviving effect.

My Yorkshire Folk in the Early 1900s

The achievement that my father was most proud of was the making of a pit-bottom rail junction for a branch tunnel. There was a points system so that corves could be sent in the particular direction required. He spent much time drawing on paper at home and went on talking about it even in bed. He laid out the lines in the yard outside his shop and I went down to see his junction. This achievement was a happy episode and a relief from the usual way in which his leisure time was spent.

The only other time when I had been down a pit was at the Battye Day-hole, so called because it was across the River Calder at a spot near where Battye had had his ferryboat. Arthur Neal, who had been a clerk at Stott's flour mill and whose sister had been one of our pupil teachers in the Infants' School, got work at the day-hole as a check-weighman. He sat in a little hut near the mouth of the day-hole, his job being to weigh every corve coming out and to credit the amount of coal to the miner whose tally hung at the corner of the corve.

Arthur was a keen churchman and once, having a message for him, I went to the day-hole. Arthur arranged for me to go down - or rather along - in this case riding in a corve, one of a train pulled by a pony. The slow journey brought the teamer and me slowly into the increasing darkness, eventually to a wide space where there was a huge fire on a kind of altar, a fine sight in contrast with the gloom of the radiating tunnels. Above the fire was an air shaft leading to the surface up on the hillside. It was a simple way of ventilating the pit. The empty waggons were shunted off and a train of full ones assembled, after which the ponyman and I sat on the coals for the return to daylight.

I always took my father's dinner to the pit when he was working over at the weekend. One Sunday I found that he was working on the headgear, the superstructure above the shaft. After Sunday School I went down to the pit again, this time with some boys. We saw my father and his mates still up there, and at a moment when I happened to be looking away, one of the boys suddenly shouted to me "Thi father's fallen!". This sadistic hoax was a terrible shock to me.

This reminds me of an accident my father had. There were occasions when he had to work over. The men required for this had mixed feelings, but there was always the pleasure of calculating how much overtime money would be added on the next Friday. My mother and I were at home. It was a dark winter's night. My father entered, weary and with face almost unrecognisable under blood and mud. He had been riding on a 'tram' (like a corve without sides) and had been thrown off. There were two seams of coal, the Black Bed and the Better Bed, and these had faults, so that there was much uphill and downhill in the pit passages. On this occasion my father had been impatient to come out and risked letting the tram run too fast. Riding required care, the tunnels being in black darkness except for the light of the safety oil-lamps carried by everyone who descended. My mother bathed my father's face and hands, and he broke no time from work.

One Sunday after he had eaten his dinner, my father persuaded the winder to let a friend and me go down the pit. The sensation when the cage was dropping at full speed in the middle of its course was unique for me. I had the feeling that my stomach. was going in the reverse direction. At the bottom we walked some way along one of the tunnels leading to the face, which by this time in the history of the pit was far from the 'pit-eye'.

Two stories occur to me from my father's time. One of the shafts was being sunk and horses were used for hauling up the big buckets of earth. A young horse came on the job, and turned restless. An attempt to make it come forward made it resist and go backwards. It fell down the shaft and was killed. On its being hauled out the navvies set to work and got meat from the horse, thoroughly enjoying the feast. They asked if the horse replacing the dead one could be a young one.

The wire rope which did the pulling up and down the pit shaft, working alternate cages, wound round a huge drum in the winding-house, with a man sitting there and regulating the amount of steam and braking as he watched a pointer moving round a dial. It was a skilled job, the amount of lever pulling varying with the time of day, whether at the beginning with down loads of men or the reverse in the afternoon, and with the loads of coal and shale. An improved system was being introduced to prevent mishap to the cage if the winder should make a mistake. An automatic device was being tested and the winder was told: "Let the cage go too far". The experiment was repeated several times unsuccessfully. In the end the man begged to be excused. His reaction to the pointer as it approached the denser mark had become automatic.

Joseph H Hird

People passing the workshop in the pit yard would loiter and peep in and get into a brief conversation with the men at work, my father and his striker at one end and the joiner at the other. All the visitors and the events in the yard could be seen by these workmen. I think the rural setting and the opportunities for incidental relief from the toil in the shop were among the reasons for my father's unwillingness to make any attempt to get other work. There was a wide variety of casual acquaintances from tramps and Irish short-time labourers in the fields, to hawkers, technicians coming for some special work at the pit and requiring some service and to gentlemen out for an afternoon stroll, one of these being the Vicar of Hartshead.

One casual caller at the workshop, a Jew, made a lucky contact. An asset desired by my father was a good watch, and watches and jewellery were this travelling salesman's line. He saw from the only half concealed interest that persistence might be worthwhile. He persuaded my father to reveal our address, saying that it would be no trouble to call in the evening and show the very thing needed for the special requirement of resistance to changes of temperature such as from the hot forge furnace to the windy yard and pit bottom. The Jew came to our house and sat on the chair near the door. There were hours of talk with cheerful irrelevancies and attempts to interest my mother in ladies' watches and jewellery. My father bought a heavy 'chronometer'. It lasted for the rest of his life. Changing over on Saturday afternoon from the cord which secured the watch in his fob pocket in his fustian trousers to his suit was an item with its set place in the moves from working clothes to leisured decency.

The patient visitor called several times in the next few years, always with the same quiet, unhurried friendliness and understatement about the object of his visit, but there was no further lapse into temptation. That watch, our sideboard, the treadle sewing-machine and the wet-battery alarm clock upstairs were the principal ones among the few capital goods in our house in the first two decades of this century. A complete inventory would have extended the list but little.

At home in the evenings my father would express himself about the laziness and self-indulgence of the masters at the pit, the dodging among the men, the unfair allotment of nasty jobs, and the wiles of men 'greasing in' with the bosses in order to get a pit-top job. The lamp job was one keenly sought. For this the lucky one had a cabin near the shaft and the miners passed his little window twice a day, early to get a safety lamp, cleaned, kindled and sealed, and again in the afternoon in the reverse direction to pass in the lamp. It could not be opened by the miner, as it had a kind of catch underneath. The lamp man put it on a stand and pressed with his foot a switch which operated a magnet to draw down a connection in the lamp and permit the bottom to be screwed off. At the end of the shift a technique of smart movement was necessary so as not to delay the waiting miners who arrived at the window in successive groups of about half a dozen as the cage brought them up. Between the beginning and the end of the shift the lamp man had an easy time in his warm cabin, cleaning the lamps and arranging them in neat rows, interrupted only by the casual appearance at his window of men (among them my father) who needed to go down on some maintenance job.

There were other pit-top jobs which were lucky in being free from the darkness and the tramping in the greasy mud of the underground passages. Two men spent their time on a platform high up on the headgear. They attended to the cage bringing up its two-tier load of full corves. These they rolled off, pushed on one side and quickly replaced with empties. The cage having then descended, they pushed the waiting corves along to the shoot where a train of waggons waited to be clamped on to the endless rope which would start them on their journey of several miles across country to Low Moor. Any brief intervals in the winding could be spent in the snug near the cage. Here miners awaiting their turn for descent gathered for a few minutes of warmth and gossip. There was another snug at the bottom for men arriving after finishing their shift. Loitering in this recess was a cause of one of my father's grumbles about men who kept him waiting for them to assist him in some repair job on the track or to inspect a correction he had made in the wiring.

The supervision of the pumping-engine was a desirable job. This was housed in a tall building with a boiler on the ground floor and a staircase leading up to the level of the arm which activated the massive rocker lowering the empty buckets and raising the full. It was with the discarded leather from these that our footwear repairs were done at home. I got to know this engine room well as it was there that I went to put my father's dinner to keep warm till he came up, on those Sundays when he had to do some repair not possible when the pit was working.

My Yorkshire Folk in the Early 1900s

A friendly engineman used to ask a few questions about the interests of 'Sam's lad', meanwhile latching the long smooth slide of the ends of the shaft into their grooves, keeping time with the 'swoosh-and-click' of the buckets going up and down on the arms of the monstrous rocker. The Three Nuns Pit was in the bottom of a wide sloping area like half a saucer and a large quantity of water was raised from the sump. Indeed, in good weather the beck running by the pit was kept flowing mainly by the supply from underground.

In the yard near my father's workshop was another engine house. Up the adjacent shaft, air was sucked in from the workings to be replaced by fresh air entering by the main shaft. Very little effort was required here, and the job had gone to Jimmy Hoyle. It was in this man's little white-washed cottage at Cooper Bridge that my father had lodged during the weeks between his appointment to the position of blacksmith and our migration from Low Moor to Mirfield. Jimmy had been unlucky. In 1900 a de-tracked corve in the pit bottom pinned him against the wall of the tunnel and crushed his leg, which had to be amputated. With his wooden leg and his sedentary habit, he became very fat and not infrequently a visitor to his engine room would find him asleep. Censure went no further than a little raillery, the payment he received being regarded more as compensation than a wage.

Three men lost their lives in roof falls in the pit during my father's time there. He was at work in his forge when one of these men was carried in. His back had been injured but his brain was lucid. There was doubt about the extent of the injury to his spine, so while the deputy talked to him a pin was stuck surreptitiously into his leg. He did not wince.

One of the most enviable jobs at the pit was that of clerk in the office. This man's work raised him a step above the men who handled rough dirty things and had dirty clothes, and whose talk had the sane crudity. In fact the man had 'collar and tie' job. He had a fine, beautiful style of handwriting. (I had plenty of evidence of this at our house when my father brought home the disused ledgers so that I could use the blank sides for writing notes.) His mental arithmetic was wonderful. Illustrating this, my father put three fingers on our table and pushed them forward to show at what speed the clerk could reckon up all the three columns at once. "And", he added for my benefit: "that's a chap 'as started working at ten."

Short visits by the clerk to the repair shop were welcome. He came to transmit orders and to receive from the joiner and my father requisitions for wood and iron. He passed on information about coming events, visits of inspectors, new machinery, a 'slap-up' dinner to order at the Three Nuns Inn, as well as references to arguments and disagreements in the office. This formed the staple of the talk between joiner and blacksmith on the clerk's return to his work, as well as being rehearsed again in our house in the evening. All this my mother and I were happy for him to do, for while my father was analysing in his crude way the doings of the bosses, we were immune from his attention. In fact, we heard interesting things, such as references to the mining map, how far and in what direction the tunnels were going, landmarks on the surface above the working points making this intelligible to us.

The Three Nuns Pit was an extension of a line of pits from Low Moor southwards. Another pit, the King's Head, was only a quarter of a mile away from our house; another large pit was at Thornhill, and there was also the day-hole across the river at Battyeford. The Three Nuns Pit, less than a mile from our house, was the remotest of that chain of the Low Moor Company's pits.

It (and the nearby inn) got its name from an adjacent building which had been a priory or convent, as was recalled by the picture over the inn door of nuns at prayer before the altar. About two hundred yards away there is an obelisk surmounted by a stone ball. It stands on a triangle at the junction with the road to Brighouse on the Huddersfield-Leeds road. The obelisk is known as the 'Dumb Steeple' ('dumb' having been 'doom' or 'judgement', as in Domesday Book). The area within a certain distance of a religious foundation had formerly offered temporary sanctuary to any fleeing criminal who could reach it without being caught. There was also a Robin Hood legend which told how Robin, ill and dying, had reached the priory, then ruled by a relative (one version says that she poisoned him for his crime of robbery). To indicate where he would like to be buried, he shot an arrow out of the window for Little John to see where it should fall. In Kirklees Park behind the inn and pit, there is a grave in an enclosure. Recorded on a tablet of stone there is the fact (if such it is) that there lie the mortal remains of Robin Hood. It was this inscription that Mr Alcock had read to us on our outing to the Park.

Joseph H Hird

The Three Nuns Pit was run almost as a family business by the three Hargreaves. Adam, the manager, was now an old man. He had started as a hurrier, so young and small that his collier had to carry him home on his back at the end of the exhausting shift. Hurriers were young lads paired with a miner (generally living with him also) for helping to move the corves particularly at junctions. There were other workers down there not engaged in loosening coal. These 'datlers' removed the away the shale and kept the tunnels clear.

Adam Hargreaves had become manager by long service and experience, but his two sons had come into the business after it became necessary to qualify for the Mining Certificate. Arthur had this, and was in effect the manager as his father could come only part time. Arthur was fully conscious of his importance. He aroused my father's retrospective wrath on those occasions when it had pleased him to come into the workshop and loudly declare what ought to be done. Any indiscreet reference to the practical iron work was the cue for the full swing of my father's contempt that evening at home.

One of the choicest stories about Arthur Hargreave's bumptiousness happened on the occasion of the arrival of some large, new machinery. When the carts and the gang of men appeared in the yard, Arthur came out of the office and took charge. This had to be put here and that there. He had it in his mind's eye just how everything was to be laid out. The accompanying men listened and looked at the pit manager, but said nothing and did nothing. It seemed to Arthur necessary to repeat more slowly and clearly what was required. He was part way through this patient exercise when a well-dressed man appeared from the cart road and, after the briefest formal introduction of himself and apology for the delay, turned to his men with his precise instructions. The 'dummies' were galvanized into action, leaving Arthur a lone unheeded spectator. All the pit-top men (including, of course, my father and his mate the joiner, and the striker) missed nothing of the scene.

The younger Hargreaves son was less concerned and energetic. He was coming into a place waiting for him in what had come to be the family management of the pit. There was ample opportunity to get to know the practical side, but the certificate was necessary and he was indolent and was having to repeat his courses of study.

It happened that at that time there was at the Three Nuns Pit a young miner ambitious to rise to management. He was doing his shift at the coal face, hurrying home, washing and changing and going to Leeds University Geology Department for evening lectures, and was passing at each stage. Travelling conditions were not easy then and the night's rest was short, but he showed no tendency to relax in attendances and settle at the pit. The Hargreaves brothers treated him with a disdainful respect.

Another pit-bottom lad, unwilling to look forward to a miner's routine of a hard day's work and an evening sitting, talking, smoking and drinking, had made himself a laughing stock on his first day arrival to be a hurrier by having cleaned his boots. One shift he went to evening classes in Huddersfield for instruction in woodwork. He left the coalface to take a position as a manual instructor in New Zealand.

13

Worsted Weaving at Learoyd's

The place of my mother's longest employment was Learoyd's. The mill was remote from our house and the means of travel so inadequate that she had a long walk, morning and evening. In winter particularly, women workers from our direction kept together on the walk, but my mother had sometimes to walk up from the bottom of the hill alone. There was a worry at one time as she was sure a man was following her in the darkness.

The routine of the journey and the weaving became second nature and my mother, more inclined to be sociable than my father was, found the company on the journey and in the loom gate a pleasant contrast with the toil and the nightly coarse grumbling at home.

There was pride in earning a reputation for being capable of weaving the most expensive cloth. Decisions about this were made by the overlooker who was in frequent, daily contact with the weavers. Selection for taking learners was also a good mark. Beside the interest in seeing their own pieces grow, there was always the need to look out for 'an end down', requiring repair with the weaver's knot. But there was time for a glance at adjacent looms and across gangways to see the next who would 'fell out'. In the din women near each other shouted, watching lip movements and signs as well. Across the gangways these latter aids to conversation were the only ones available.

As dinnertime approached the loom would be stopped for the short journey to the oven if there was anything to warm. A little rice pudding in an earthenware dish or a bit of leftover meat pie were the treats for the days when the meal was not bread and butter and tea. For her tea, by the way, my mother had a two-lidded can with tea at one end and sugar at the other.

In the weaving shed there was a human interest which my mother would have missed if she had stayed at home, there being little 'neighbouring' at that time from our house. The women weavers came to the mill from a wide area round Huddersfield and benefited from being able to tell their troubles to their nearest friends as they sat in little groups of their choice in the loom gate during the dinner hour.

In the evening there was a contrast between my father's loud, blustering, oath-strewn grumbling and my mother's gentler, usually pleasant gossip from the mill. She talked about the kind of piece she had in, when she would probably fell out and be able to 'fettle' (clean up, though for thorough cleaning there were men fettlers), whose loom was standing, and wondering why that weaver was missing, some young weaver going to get married, another wishing she could stay at home, somebody scolded for loitering in the lavatory (not the word my mother used).

There were special occasions. In 1905 the mill was trimmed for the centenary of the Battle of Trafalgar, after which the mill was named. All work stopped on another occasion when a new engine was named. The oldest weaver was Elizabeth, and at the ceremony she gave the engine her name. Now and again masters would stroll round with visitors and guests.

A few times a shuttle flew out. A kind of rod at each end of the loom, attached with a leather strap, jerked the shuttles across between the threads of the warp, which jumped up and down to form the particular pattern required. The shuttles entered boxes to wait for a moment before being jerked back again, the speed of the transit being too quick for the eye. On one occasion a woman was seriously injured by an escaping shuttle.

My mother would tell us her tales pleasantly while doing her housework, and so long as my parents kept to their work stories the evening passed tolerably, but not when their views and criticisms turned towards each other. Then there were terrible rows, my mother's voice rising with my father's in mutual recrimination. Unless I was playing out with the neighbouring children, I had to be the lonely witness of these rows from the time I was eight.

I have referred to my mother's friendliness with other Learoyd's women. A few times this got as far as our visiting them on a Saturday afternoon. This required some per-suasion at home, as my father did not like visiting. Once my parents put on their Sunday clothes and went with me on a Saturday visit to a house in

Leeds Road not far from the mill. We got no answer from the door and had to come home. My father was furious about the trouble we had taken.

We did have tea with one woman and her family at Huddersfield and again with the same woman when she was married. She then lived at the Bradley Bar House on top of the hill leading from Brighouse and over to Sheepbridge and Fartown for Huddersfield. When I have in later years ridden to Huddersfield on the bus, it has recurred to my memory that I once sat at tea in a room on the very spot which is now part of a busy roundabout. In earlier days vehicles had had to pause there to pay toll.

Another visit, a very pleasant one, was to Annie Wainwright's at Kirkburton. There were two sisters and the father was the verger of the church which we visited. There was a large garden with orchard and beehives. These women, by the way, came into Huddersfield to get the tram, via the railway. There was a little train which went to and fro on this short journey and the engine was known as 'Burton Dick'.

Other personal connections were the two young women I have mentioned, my mother's learners. I do not remember the name of the bonny one. In the other case we paid a visit to the Thorntons. They lived at Bradley, and there was an effort at playing together with violin and piano.

Joseph H Hird

14

Quarrels, Lights and Noises

When before the age of eight I had the weekend at home, it was the most risky time for dissension. There would be quarrelling about troubles in the past which I could not understand. On one occasion my mother put her hat on and set off up the hill with the intention of walking back to Bradford. There was silence in the house as my father and I sat still, wondering, but my mother came back after a long interval. I think she knew that it would be futile to expect any consolation from anyone related to her.

On another occasion they for some reason or other quarrelled over me. I had done nothing. The trouble was in their own minds and memories. It came to each one grabbing one of my arms and engaging in a tug-of-war. I was bewildered and crying, and my mother was shouting incoherently through her sobs over my head.

214

My Yorkshire Folk in the Early 1900s

My father's criticisms of the pit managers (for such things as signing to say they had inspected underground, when they had in fact not left the office) was a monologue, but unfortunately he thought he had reason to criticise my mother also, as he reclined tilted back in his cratch while she worked on the week's tasks. One Monday evening during the washing she became angry at his remarks and flung the block of soap at his head. It hit him on the bridge of his nose. He was so taken aback that he became silent.

These rows, most often occurring on Sunday, would go on to the point of weariness and move towards a conclusion by my father's seeking a mild cause of complaint which my mother could easily deal with as if it had arisen only out of a misunderstanding. My father could then make the move he was secretly wanting to make:"If tha'd nobbut said that afoor", and bedtime would come with my father using the only term of endearment he ever used: "Doy". (I think this word must have been a Yorkshireman's nearest venture to Darling.)

Three years after my return home from the Copleys' I had started having homework to do. My father felt that this was important, being part of the scheme which he had conceived on my admission to the Grammar School. He had two desks made by the joiner at work. One was large enough to hold books and have a ledge for an inkwell and there was a small one to rest my book on. Both were useless, but he felt he had done something to help, and he had taken a risk in having them made and in bringing them home.

How fortunate it was that these appropriations of company's materials and time were not discovered! Dismissal could easily have been the consequence, with an abrupt end to my schooling if I had had to get a job. It was known that the bosses had things made out of the firm's materials, but it is doubtful whether the knowledge that he had worked for the bosses would have saved an employee of much lower status such as my father.

The evenings I have described made it clear that I could not continue the attempt to do homework downstairs, so I had to retire upstairs. In winter it was cold and dark up there but I wrapped my legs up and later kindled a fire. When I went upstairs to study, light was obtained at first from a small oil lamp on a nail on the wall. It had come from the pit and was inadequate. My eyes suffered from it. A time came when I had to sit up there for several hours together, and often my eyes were already tired by trying to read in the train dimly lit by gas on the journey from Leeds. I did homework upstairs in these conditions up to finishing at the University, with a change from oil lamp to gas when this was extended up through the floor. Still there was but a poor light with the old-fashioned gas mantle, but I benefited by getting out of the way of the talk downstairs, which from then on distracted my attention only when it reached a certain pitch of violence.

I have made reference to the use of a candle for 'going round the back'. The candlestick was much in use at our house. It was carried upstairs, into the little cellar, and out to the coalplace. My father had the funny idea of giving me a copper tube with which I could blow out the candle when I had tucked myself up in bed. It was about three-foot-six in length, and I kept it propped up near the bedhead. Of course it had come from the pit.

For downstairs lighting we had an oil lamp suspended over the table and under a circular piece of paper with a design stuck on the ceiling. This had a varnished surface, so that the soot rising from the lamp could be wiped off. The taking down, trimming the wick, washing the glass chimney and the white shade, brightening of the brasswork, and filling up with paraffin were a Saturday evening's activity of my mother's. I went fairly frequently up the hill to the house of Sam Ledgard, who came out and went with me to his hut in the yard to fill my paraffin can. I liked the smell of the hut, a smell consisting of a mixture of firewood, firelighters and paraffin. It never occurred to me what an immediate tremendous conflagration would have burst out if there had been only a slight error with the light.

The light from our oil lamp was not good, particularly on the spot where it was most needed ie on the table immediately below. In the design of the lamp there was some sort of provision for throwing the light downwards by having a kind of white inverted dish to sit on the shoulder of the funnel (this latter being necessary to make the light bright by forcing the air to rush vertically past the wick). But we still had a large round dark area on the table.

There was a gasworks at Ravensthorpe and piping was extending from it into our area and into houses. My father did not favour changes at that time, but my mother nattered and eventually went with me one day to the gas office and enquired about the possibility of having it installed. This was one of the rare instances of my mother getting her way.

There was great excitement when we learnt that there was enough demand to justify laying a pipe. The work took place when I was on holiday and could give access to the house. With a penny-in-the-slot meter under the sink, the need to admit the gasman with his tool for opening and his leather bag for the load of coppers was an inconvenience we had not experienced when we had oil lighting. But we got a brighter light from the gas mantel, at first upright and then inverted, thus eliminating for the first time the dark circle on the table. Other advantages followed in time. The early morning drink of cocoa taken before my parents started their long walk had had for many years to be made with water boiled on firewood. A gas-ring was a wonderful improvement, but caused increased expense, for the firewood had cost nothing, neither had our coal, except the five shillings for carting.

Some years after I had left home my father paid for electricity to be installed. He wanted mains current for his wireless set, giving him enough power to make a great din, which delighted him. He liked to have the set on with the door wide open so as to make passers-by look and, as he thought, admire his powerful set. I was sitting in the house one afternoon when two of the Resurrection Fathers came up the hill on their afternoon walk. They were, of course, walking in the middle of the road. I saw them stop talking and stare with a frown at our door as they walked past. Incidentally, I remember that the Father preaching at a quarry service soon after the introduction of religious broadcasting said that no one would ever be converted by that means.

My Yorkshire Folk in the Early 1900s

My father had great pride in electricity, because of the power it gave him, and the consciousness that, having bought some shares in the Yorkshire Electric Power Company, he was part owner of the supply. Of course, with this modernisation, the contemptible gas was eliminated from the house. Heating of water in the brass kettle and some cooking were done on a small flat circle stove. No further progress in lighting or heating, such as a radiator or a hot-water tap, was made. To the end of my time and, indeed, to the end of my father's days and my mother's stay in that house, I and my mother used a zinc bath kept under the bed upstairs. This itself was an improvement, for I had had to continue to stand in the baking bowl to be washed by my mother, till sometime after I thought I could have washed myself, but she wished to reduce the amount of water scattered about.

My father did not have a full wash down, but stripped to the waist on Saturday dinnertime and washed down to his middle with the assistance of my mother or me to wash his back. He changed his shirt, put on a linen collar and a tie, the collar worn without a tie during the week having been a composition one and dark with sweat and grease. The weekly shave took place on Saturday afternoon, with a cut-throat razor. (I also began my shaving with that kind of razor; it was not till 1920 that I acquired a safety razor.) My father continued the washing, to complete the lower half, on his return from his Saturday night out. I had been able to use the bath behind a clothes-horse, and while my mother took a bath I went upstairs to occupy myself till she called me down.

Our house was not adequate for a family, even where there was only one child. This was especially evident in the lack of sleeping accommodation. My bed on the landing was very close to that of my parents. It was often wrongly assumed that if I was in bed I was asleep, but this was not always so, and I had to hear things said and done which were unsuitable for young ears.

As well as quarrelling and digging up past reproaches, there was evidence of the part that sex played in such narrow lives. How unfair this was to my mother. She rose at five o'clock to set off after having a drink of cocoa, on her long walk to the tram, with a long day's work to follow, and then return to do homework which lasted till eleven o'clock or later. Yet even that short night was not all available for the much needed rest. I cannot understand how she endured so long. At intervals she had violent headaches and would go to bed to have cloths soaked in vinegar laid along her forehead, but she did not break time from work. As for me, I cannot describe the effect of those nights on me, not daring to make any sound for fear of what might happen to me if I destroyed the wilful illusion that I was soundly asleep.

That way of behaving may to some extent be accounted for by the conditions under which my father had been brought up. In his family there were six children huddled together with their parents in a low-decker cottage, and there was little else in their lives but work and coarse, physical indulgences, of which sex was the keenest and the cheapest, as well as being the least evident to outsiders and the most constantly available.

There was little education, and no vision of a use of leisure which might have reduced the drag downwards. My father's father was a drinker and a gambler, but my father went to no clubs or pubs. His keenness about money safeguarded him from these vices, leaving a concentration on indulgence in violent use of the tongue, gluttony, and the pleasure of the bed. The situation at our house seems to have resembled that in which my father had spent his youth. Annie's mother, brought up a few yards from my grandparents' house, was familiar with the sight of members of the Hird family (she was of about the same age as the oldest child, my Uncle Joe), and told me that my grandmother always looked weary and harassed.

My situation must have been far from unique amongst my schoolmates in the Elementary School. This may account for the contrast between the pious repetitions we were accustomed to in church and Sunday School and the quiet realism learnt at home and in the school yard. At the same time there were, in the church prayers and psalms, words which bridged the gap between piety and the crude gratification of the flesh. We acknowledged ourselves to be 'miserable sinners' and asked for deliverance from 'fornication and all other deadly sins...the flesh and the devil'.

Our house was at one corner of a block of four. We were on the roadside. The two houses at the back had more than one sleeping place, but the house at our side had, like ours, only one bedroom. For some years in my boyhood that house was occupied by a family called Lee. There was one child, a girl, older than me. Mr Lee was a blustering, coarse man, and the girl's character was evidently harmed by such restricted accommodation as we had also next door. She took a malicious pleasure in the dark, winter nights, when neighbouring boys and girls were mooning idly about in the yard and the shed under the currier's shop, in trying to thrill us with her furtive, lascivious whispering.

It was necessary to mention these things in order to account adequately for the worries with which I could hardly cope in my youth about my present situation and my future career.

I have already told of the inconvenience of sharing the place at the far end of their garden with our back-to-back neighbours. There was also some difficulty because their house and ours backed onto each other. The wall near the top of the short flight of steps leading to our little cellar was only thinly boarded up and it was easy to hear raised voices through it. We knew when there was a row on, and they at the back must have had an ample fund of topics for conversation from the turbulent events on our side.

There were other difficulties with the proximity of our neighbours. Our first rear neighbours were the Walkers. The father was a fearsome boozer. He kept a large black dog which attacked me on my way round the back. My mother took me round to the house and dropped my breeches to show the effect of the bite into my buttocks There was a grudging promise to control the animal, but for the rest of the life of that dog, the risk was a nuisance added to that of having to go round there at all.

My Yorkshire Folk in the Early 1900s

Walker senior died and left two sons, Herbert and Leonard. Both were cobblers, as I have described. Leonard was for many years a member of our Christ Church choir, at the alto end of one side. Herbert married and stayed on as our rear neighbour. A daughter was born, the cause of some friction with us. A cradle was kept in their bedroom, and the loud bumping of this as it was rocked from the bed during the night led to a complaint from my parents. The most striking effect of the insufficient insulation between the two houses was Herbert's gastric ulcer. The crisis of this caused him to yell without intermission, and we had no peace till he was taken away.

They were an unfortunate family. The daughter seemed to get the rocking into her system and wanted to do nothing during her childhood but oscillate in the rocking-chair. She, like Mrs Crawshaw our roadside neighbour, was taken to a lunatic asylum. Herbert's bad health induced him to drown himself in a large tub near his shop.

As we had a coal fire, there was a fairly frequently recurring necessity to sweep the chimney, and this had to be done partly from the house at the back. In their little attic there were two lids in the wall, giving access to the flues. The part of the chimney adjacent to these holes was almost horizontal, and in time soot accumulated in such quantity that the reduced draught caused a dull fire and smoke returning to the living-room. My father swept our chimney and this required permission for access to our rear neighbour's garret. They did not like giving consent to go into their bedrooms, and a little dirt was inevitable. In times of social coolness a blunt statement of inconvenience was a way of reproof, and we had to put up with unsatisfactory heating till it seemed suitable to make another contact.

We did not have adequate material to cover our big open hearth for when the huge mass of soot would shutter down, and the idea occurred that we might try to get the services of a professional chimney-sweep who might cause less dirt in our house and be better able to get permission to go into the garret at the back.

There was such a man in Nab Lane, living in a row of houses called The Wasp's Nest. His name was Entwistle. There were children of his in our school, and rough and bold they were. I went to the house to see him, and was told to go and ask for him at The Mooky Dook. This would have been called officially, I believe, The Stocks Bank Workingmen's Club, but it was only a low-decker at the far end of a yard. It took some time for him to come to the door after my enquiry. He did not wish to be bothered; he did not know when he could come.

We gave up the idea of having the services of a professional sweep. Mr Entwistle had a monopoly of that occupation in our area, but he preferred to booze in the Mooky Dook rather than accept commissions. When he was out he was to be seen sitting on his flat cart with his supply of sacks and sacking, complacently moving along at the pace chosen by the anaemic donkey. It was no more interested in arriving at the destination than was its master behind, indifferently looking round while sucking at the stub of his clay pipe.

15

Village Traffic

In writing about the 'gentry' earlier I have mentioned some of the farms near Hill Top. Another, further up the hill was the Farrers' farm. Three of the Farrers lived there, all unmarried. David was the farmer proper, though he ran another business, cattle dealer, as well. John, who did very little on the farm, was a secretary at Crowther's mill, the one which burnt down so gloriously one night. John's passing our door was one of the clockwork routines of our day. Miss Farrer did the domestic side, serving milk and eggs, and attending to the poultry. A man was employed to work in the fields and attend to the cows.

My father sent me a few times to the Farrers' farm to buy a young cock, but this stopped after one we got was found to have suffered some injury or disease and had a big lump of corrupt flesh in it.

I visited the farm regularly in mid-week to fetch our extra quart of milk, for my mother believed it necessary to make bread right. I often arrived before the milking had been done, and was allowed to leave my jug in the kitchen and go along into the mistal. I used to watch the farmhand milking, which was done in conditions that now horrify me to think of. The mistal had a very strong smell and was thickly bespattered with dung along the floor and on the walls, the khaki coloured coating of the dried splashes diminishing and merging into the faded whitewash as one's eye moved up the wall. The cows themselves were caked with dung, and the milking was unhygienic. The man did not wash his hands before applying them to the teats. If the cow fidgeted he slapped its filthy side before resuming the milking. The milk was poured into a big can with a handle, from the big vessel with a rim which the man had held between his knees while he sat at the udder on his three-legged stool. The can was at the end of the row of milkers, and then carried into the farm kitchen stone sink where the water supply came via a pump.

The milk was passed into my jug through a funnel, at the bottom of which was a sieve which became partly clogged up with dirt and hairs. I watched Miss Farrer, who sometimes during this operation spoke to me politely in good English while she measured out my quart. If the milk was poured off carefully at home some dirt remained at the bottom of the jug. Our regular daily pint, brought to the door in a big can over the edge of which hung a gill (half-pint) measure and a pint measure, did not leave much dirt at the bottom of our pint basin, as we rarely got the dregs from the can. We had little concern about such things (the word *unhygienic* was unknown to us).

My Yorkshire Folk in the Early 1900s

The Farrers' farm was much smaller than the one at Fieldhead, and David Farrer was not a very approachable man. He had a reputation as a drinker. I would see him back from his cattle dealing, sitting in the kitchen, a bare sort of place with a stone sink containing a water pump and filter, with nothing to cover the stone floor. Huddled in the uncomfortable kind of bare, wooden chair, semi-circular for arm and back rest, with bars connecting to the seat (and curiously called a *cratch*), he rested his stocking feet on the ledge at the bottom of the oven door. I was nervous of his gruff presence.

I had got to know the Farrers' farmhand, as he finished work at the time in the evening that I had to walk to Heckmondwike for a violin lesson, and we kept each other company on the dark country roads. He was an amateur boxer and told me about his great future.

A morning duty of the farmhand was to carry round milk in a can with a measure suspended on the rim, for pouring into the housewife's basins to measure out, just as did the milkman who called at our house to deliver one pint into a basin left outside the door when we were not in. The farmhand only delivered to certain customers, chiefly at Highthorpe, up Slipper Lane. I did this task for the nine mornings of his absence as a territorial. David Farrer paid me one shilling and sixpence. I had earned about tuppence a day, but that was a windfall for me.

In spring we knew for a wide distance round the farm when a certain operation was in progress. Outside, next to the mistal there was a submerged tank with a pipe leading down into it. Through this pipe ran an endless chain with flanges fitting the inside. At the right season the man turned the wheel over which the chain passed and the liquid manure was lifted, to run along a channel into a huge barrel on a cart. The liquid was to be spread on the grass fields. It was so ripe with its long process of maturing that the smell was overpowering as one approached on the causeway which ran within a few yards of the pouring liquids. The Farrers had a fine crop of hay.

Horses dominated road traffic till well on in my youth. There was Dr Elwell who visited up our hill. He had a handsome horse which pulled an open, four-seater carriage, two opposite two, a landau. In good weather the doctor's round must have had much pleasure mixed with duty.

The heavy, hard-working carthorses needed frequent replacements of their shoes, and the shoesmiths had their smithies in our village. Near a junction in our parish a smithy stood near an inn called The Horseshoe. We knew the smith, not only from looking in at his wide-open door when he had a horse inside, but also because he took his turn as a Sunday School superintendent. The limitation of his physique made his work hard. He was a little man. One leg was straight, while the other was curved almost to a semi-circle, which suggests that he had begun to bear the weight of a horse's leg before his bones had been fully set.

Another job needed with the use of carthorses was that of the wheelwright. There was a wheelwright's yard opposite the smithy. The construction of a cart (by a 'cartwright') was a highly skilled job, particularly in shaping the wheels out of very hard wood, with use of that tool, now almost extinct, the spoke shave. I watched how the iron tyres were fitted, when the hub, spokes and felloes were all in place. A spacious fire was kindled from fragments of wood and shavings in the open yard. The wheel was ready, propped up on a stand. The iron tyre already fitted the wheel but was just a little short in circumference. Then the tyre was put on the fire, the heat of which would cause it to expand. When quite hot, the tyre was transferred to the waiting wheel, adjusted correctly. The whole wheel was lifted off quickly for the wood was beginning to char and dropped into a large tank of water. The consequent contraction gave a tightness which would grip the wheel and last a very long time.

Horses were much used by street traders also. On Saturday afternoons the greengrocer's cart would come up the hill. Tom Sheard gave plenty of warning of his approach. His shouted list of the contents of his cart could be heard a hundred yards away. This was useful because it gave time for a brief discussion in our house as to whether there was to be 'ought' or 'nought'. If my mother did not soon appear when the cart stopped opposite our door, Tom would stroll round his horse giving it irrelevant caresses and making a show of adjustments to the harness, meanwhile re-shouting his list and looking vaguely about, anywhere but at our door. According to the decision on that particular Saturday, my mother would go to the door and call out: "Nought today, Tom!:" or go out into the road wiping her hands and gathering up her apron to make a temporary bag with it.

Tom's business was interfered with. An enterprising young greengrocer, Harry Wright, from Hartshead, with a bigger cart and a younger horse than Tom's, decided to extend his round and appeared from the top side of our hill. My mother gave way to the temptation to go to his cart and "Nought today, Tom!" became more frequent.

One Saturday the new greengrocer had not forestalled his rival, and as the two carts drew nearer we wondered what would be the outcome of the meeting between the established man and the usurper. Like two armies of former times they approached within speaking range, each man holding his horse's head, and as if by agreement, stopped at about twenty yards from each other, left their vehicles and met in no man's land to parley. They were both decent fellows (I met Harry Wright some years later in the house of some nice people at Hartshead when I had gone to try duets with the son, and Harry was there on a courting visit to the sister). They came to a peaceful settlement, which cannot have been very satisfactory for the older man. The young man would leave Saturday to Tom, but would show that he himself was entitled to come that way by coming on the Friday evenings. He knew, of course, that a visit in mid-week would not have been worthwhile. All the working people were paid on Fridays.

A different sort of cart came occasionally. It was called the 'pot cart' and was heavily loaded with a variety of things useful in the house. Besides all the mugs, plates, bowls, jugs and chamber pots there were metal things: pans, kettle, baking tin, cans; and there were brushes of all sorts and candles and tapers, clothes-pegs, ruddle and firelighters. Many of the metal things were suspended from the roof of the cart, causing a musical jingle as the cart moved along over the dross-covered road. In the darkness of the winter evening these carts were a cheerful centre of illumination. A bright oil lamp, slung from the roof of the cart, shed light not only on the stacked-up goods on the cart, but also on the surrounding black area of the road. In the rear part of the cart there was a large tank of paraffin with tap projecting out at the back, so that a measuring can could be suspended from it. At the rear end of the cart also was a large sack for rags and discarded clothes. For these an allowance was made against purchases.

Now and again on cold winter nights in winter a cry was to be heard: 'Pays (peas) all 'ot!' and a basin could be taken out to make an extra meal of this trouble-free indulgence.

A man from Bank Street carrying his produce in a large wicker basket on his arm used to come up the hill on a morning mid-week, a suitable time for the baking. He was selling yeast. A bell dangling from the edge of the basket automatically announced his approach. When a woman came out he lifted the white cloth and raised brass scales by the ring above the centre of the balance arm. The scale pans each dropped to the extent of the triple chains. He had a small set of brass weights on which he weighed the yeast broken off from the lump in its hempen sack.

He also came round on Friday mornings, this time to sell freshly made oatcakes made in elliptical shapes of about 12 inches by 6. When I was at home in the holidays I seized the opportunity to go out with the necessary coppers to buy one. I was impatient for a reasonable dinnertime to arrive, so that I could spread treacle and make a roll, biting one end and then the other to catch the treacle. The oatcake made a delicious sandwich for an entire meal. Annie's mother used to go down from Low Moor to Oakenshaw for these havercakes. There was a relative there skilled in making them. This woman used to rise early to get the 'bakst'n' (bake-stone) up to the right heat while preparing the mixture of oatmeal and water. Knowing the right amount for these went along with skill in throwing the mixture with a spatula on to the bake-stone and to get the cake off in one piece only just baked though and slightly brown on one side. At Low Moor Aunt Rose sometimes dried the oatcakes on the 'breeadflag' (bread-flag) and we dipped fragments in butter.

Another trader was Tommy Bickerdike. He hawked pomatum for the hair. His cry was "Ony pom!" To supply other small things needed by housewives other hawkers came round with a box suspended from the shoulders. When the lid was raised, the multiplicity of what was stored was remarkable: pins, needles, scissors, ribbons, elastic, cotton reels, cards of darning wool, thimbles – all neatly stowed under a few small towels and handkerchiefs.

Scissor grinders passed, pushing the simple machine on a big wheel. The front could be lowered to give a stable position. A rope round an extra wheel at the side of the big wheel connected with the little grinding wheel. A footboard, as on a spinning wheel for wool, activated the big wheel and the difference in size produced a high-speed revolution for grinding. The whole structure was not heavy. The grinder announced his approach with: "Shears to grind! Scissors, knives to sharpen!" Later a more up-to-date way came as an adapted bicycle.

At our house we needed no such aid, for my father as a worker in iron had all the skill necessary; he easily kept our scissors and knives sharp. A more delicate sharpening was required for his cut-throat razor, which he ground from time to time on a smooth stone, with oil, and every week with a strop, necessary after a week's accumulation of beard.

Of the traffic on our hill it was the horses that had the most impact. In the pre-tarmac days the horses dug their toes into the surface. Heavy falls of rain washed the soil out. A carthorse pulling a load of coal up the hill had to zig-zag from side to side. By making the climb longer the gradient was reduced and both the man holding the horse's head and the animal itself stopped for a rest half-way up. For descending with a heavy load, the weight was too great for the horse to have remained on its feet. So there was a shoe, with chain, slung on a hook at the side. These carts stopped in front of our house for the shoe to be unslung and brought down in front of a wheel. (This method could only be applied to a rear wheel of a four-wheeled cart.) Thus on descending one wheel did not rotate and, with the friction on the road plus the hub brakes tightly applied in front by a rod turning them tight with a handle, the cart could descend. In slippery conditions after snow, the descent remained hazardous and the shoes themselves made the road more slippery. I have seen a horse with its back sloping and its back legs skidding forwards.

Such wear and tear on the roads required repair. This was interesting to watch. At the side of the road at the bottom of our hill, loads of dross arrived from the iron works at Low Moor. The material, which had been used in the stacks for the preparation of pure iron from the ore, was broken when solidified into lumps weighing up to the limit of what a man could lift. A long dump was made at the side of our road. It provided work for a dross-breaker for several weeks. Equipped with hammers, heavy and lighter, and wearing goggles, he started at one end and, as the days went by, the gap he made between the heap of small lumps suitable for putting on the road and that of the untouched big lumps progressed slowly.

A heavy coal-heated steam roller first scraped the surface loose and then the broken dross was scattered, to be rolled in with a mixture of dirt as the roller went to and fro. I watched the process in front of our house. The news had apparently not reached our Local Authority, the Urban District Council, that the red flag was no longer necessary, so a man had the easy task of walking in front of the roller, and then resuming his patrol on the other side when the roller reversed. Such a slow-moving structure would seem to have never had the need of the warning red flag which had been used for the first motorcars. These road repairs provided a permanent open air career of work, for the dross was not firm.

Coming back to horse traffic, Annie's father remembered the stage coach which stopped at The British Queen in Huddersfield Road, Low Moor, the guard blowing his horn. The barn at Broad Ings Farm in Shelf housed a stage coach.

I have referred to Mr Wormald's horse cab and the whipping I got from the coachman. A near miss of injury occurred one Saturday afternoon in hot, still weather. Half-way down our hill a cart-horse was standing unattended within the shafts. I was mooning about and thought I would like to be friendly so I went and patted its neck. I must have interrupted its siesta, for it raised the forefoot on my side and stamped. I felt the blow glance off my foot, a very near miss of a crushed foot.

Passengers and Waggonettes

A little way above our house was a cart drive entrance to a small farm. It was at the house along there that George Walker and Sons currier's business had developed as a kind of domestic industry in an adjoining outhouse, now used as a stable. The people living there ran a carting business, along with a few pigs and poultry as a side line. An experiment was to run a small waggonette service between the Black Bull in the centre of Mirfield and the tram terminus at Ravensthorpe to connect with the public service to Dewsbury, a distance of about a mile. My father and I went once in this vehicle. The owner would take even one passenger who might wish to avoid walking after leaving the tram from Dewsbury. We had got off the tram and, of course, were well known to the man hoping for a fare. The journey took about the same time as it would have done to have walked. This evening and Saturday work was overtime for the horse and it was not keen about it. An advantage of the service was that though the vehicle was open, there was good protection for the legs under a water proof cloth, and the
ride was an opportunity for neighbourly gossip with the driver. Our neighbour's project failed.

For his heavy hauling there was a fine white horse called Prince, I think the tallest horse I have ever seen. It used to be taken down the hill

to a field to grass. I wanted to ride on this horse and walked down several times alongside before venturing to ask. I was given a leg up but the man inconsiderately stimulated the horse to trot. The fearful bouncing made me lose my balance and I found myself ignominiously embracing the animal's neck and slipping down one side, hoping fervently that somehow I might reach the ground without injury from the drop or from the horse's hoofs. The horse was brought back to a walk in time for me to fall clumsily but safely to the ground.

We had a great affection for Bess, a black mare owned by Ledgard, a little further up the road, who sold me the paraffin for our lamp. He had a coal and furniture removal business. Bess used to come back to the hill at the end of her day's work. She pulled so vigorously up the hill to get back to food that she had to be restrained.

I had a mishap with a horse one morning on the way to the Nab School. At that time a milk-float stopped near our house to deliver milk before proceeding to the next customer at the bottom of the Nab, a little way beyond the entrance to our schoolyard. The milkman, employee of a farm at Hartshead about two miles away, was in a hurry to get round. It was astonishing that the farmer took the trouble to send so little milk so far. I got permission to ride down the hill with the milkman, and at first stayed in the float till the horse stopped its gallop. Then I ventured one morning to jump off as the vehicle passed the school entrance. I went flying forward, but saved my head by throwing out my hands. I was arriving at school much earlier than necessary, so I was able to collect myself and get into the porch to wash my bloody, dirty hands and scrape mud off my coat. The milkman did not slow down when I fell; he merely glanced at my predicament. My coat was not torn, so there was no need to say anything in the evening.

I had not learnt my lesson about getting rides. Years after that I was going to Norristhorpe, Heckmondwike, for a lesson, one evening when it was quite dark and I had reached Mirfield Moor. I stalked a lorry and, clinging to my violin case, I scrambled up at the back. The speed of motor traffic was much lower in those days. I rode till I was approaching the end of the lane where I had to turn right. I had not foreseen the difficulty of getting off. The road now dipped slightly on the long decline towards Liversedge and the speed had increased, but I had to get off. I lowered myself and started the running motion with big strides touching the road. I had to let go. I went staggering forward as anxious for the violin as for myself. I rolled on the road but prevented the violin case from being damaged or myself from having any skin broken. I was dirty and shaken and did badly in my music lesson at Mr Allenby's.

In the days of horse traffic it was a common trick amongst rough lads to steal rides, particularly if there was room to run behind as the vehicle had just passed, grab the ledge and jump up to hide behind piled-up loads. They were betrayed sometimes with the cry "Whip behind!". Some boys were daring enough to jump on even when the driver could see, if the waggon was too long for the whip to reach the back. They knew that if the man took the trouble to stop his horse and get down with his whip, they would be beyond reach of any other action than his curses, which were part of the fun.

I was exceptionally foolish in this matter of stealing vehicular assistance. Even in my early twenties, when I was returning from a cycle trip to York and feeling rather tired, I looked round at a light lorry coming up a gentle incline, to gauge the distance and the right moment to grab. My motive must have been obvious to the driver and his mate. They allowed me to grab and then put on such speed that holding and steering were too much for me and I was thrown into the gutter. The lorry disappeared round a bend, but by the time I had pulled myself together and gone on again, I saw that the driver had stopped and his mate had got out to took back. They watched me pedalling slowly; I was going to avoid the humiliation of having the lesson put into words, but I had learnt it. The construction of modern transport vehicles, their speed, and the greatly increased density of traffic have safeguarded youth from the sort of folly I have been describing.

A propos of waggonette trips, there were short ones like that for our Sunday School, but for grown-ups greater distances were undertaken. One favourite for a full day trip was to The Isle of Skye, an inn on the Pennines between

Huddersfield and Lancashire; another was Mont Sarah's and there was Bill o' Jack's. I never went on such a trip; they were arranged mainly by men's clubs.

The long ride in the fresh air sharpened appetites for a hearty meal with plenty of beer to follow, the merry crowd enlivening the return in the evening with songs and stories. Some were very lively when the party was large enough to engage several waggonettes with the sexes mixed. The return journey in on-coming dusk seemed to stimulate a desire to sing. By that time friends were fully relaxed and laughter and jokes came freely. Movement on wheels shows similar effects in the modern coach party, but the waggonette broadcast its hilarity. We have been in bed late on a Saturday night in summer and been not unpleasantly disturbed by the crescendo, forte and diminuendo of 'chapel lot' musically concluding an outing, accompanied by the syncopating clatter of the horses' hooves.

I believe there was more fun on such excursions than there is now usually on coach trips, when the passengers are a chance collection of strangers who have responded to an advertisement. The destination then was of less interest than the ride itself, and it had its variations of speed from the slow toil uphill to the jolly clip-clop of the horses trotting on the level or down a gentle slope. There was time to look at the scenery and watch it merge from the familiar into the unfamiliar and the reverse in the evening. The kind of liquid refreshment indulged in caused little worry about safety on the return journey.

Large waggonettes had a special seat for a second man of the crew. This was at the middle of the back. This man's job was to turn the little wheel at the end of a wormed shaft with gearing for the brakes on the rear wheels.

There had to be some turn-over in the supply of horses. Breaking in young horses was a cruel business. The uncomprehending young thing was driven round and round on a rope, a man in the middle applying the whip to make it keep going and teach it to respond to the pull on the bit. Whips were in frequent use and a bad-tempered or impatient horseman was a torment. The intelligent man could use the reflex action to make the voice a substitute for the whip. There used to be a pleasure vehicle, like a low, enclosed up-to-the shoulders waggonette, commonly called a governess car, passing about our roads. The gentleman riding in this had trained his horse to such a standard of reflex action that he needed only to rattle the whip, stuck at his side, upright in its socket, and the horse leapt forward.

The use of a private vehicle not merely as a matter of saving time but also avoiding being exposed to common contacts was often shown in the days of the horse-cab. These had a window at each side, permitting either complete privacy or, when open, a view and some exposure to the outside. Cab horses were not much given to hurrying and it was often as easy to walk as fast.

An excuse for ladies riding in a cab was that their sweeping skirts could pick up so much dirt or dust before tarmacadam was introduced. Skirts at that time were so long that a lady had to carry an armful of skirt as she walked, with a risk of exposing an ankle if she had to go upstairs or mount the step of a cab.

Cabbies spent a large part of their working lives in their hut at the station while their horses drowsed outside with the three accessories of nosebag, heap of dung and attendant sparrows.

I think my last experience of passenger transport by waggonette was from Hucklow to Haddon Hall in 1919 with Annie, Winifred Bishop (Freddie), her sister Dorothy and a young man also staying at Little Hucklow with the Unitarian minister, a very pleasant journey. We had also done the journey to Hucklow by waggonette from the nearest station. That holiday was the first I had ever had ie longer than the annual church day-trip.

By the time the next holiday came at Hebden in 1921, the motor charabanc with hood for rain and wheels with solid rubber tyres had come into more general use, initiating the small family businesses now swallowed up in the big companies, which in their turn are now tending to come under unified, governmental control.

I remember no more contact with horses till I went to Carlton Farm, near Nun Monkton, where my schoolboy son Brian was helping with

the harvest during the Second World War. I
helped with gathering the corn. Having gone to
take my bicycle for Brian to get to the big house
some miles away from where the school party
was accommodated, I found I could not return
home in the evening by public transport from
that remote spot. I returned to the farm for a
working visit. For the journeys between fields and
corn stack, Brian harnessed and managed the
horse like a habituated farmer's man.

Butchering

I include here further references to treatment of
animals. In a field on Kitson Hill Common
rabbit coursing took place. The activity was wide
open to view and there was no restriction on the
curiosity of the public. The rabbits, which were
numerous, had little chance to escape, though the
field was the usual sort of meadow, surrounded
by walls over which a rabbit might have jumped.
The whippet owners evidently thought that
unlikely, as the distance of release of the rabbit
and the speed of the dogs made it almost certain
that the result would be within view.

The point of the game seemed to be to gamble on the likely winner, proved by first seizure of the victim. The events proceeded in rapid succession. The caught rabbit was quickly withdrawn from the jaws of its disputing captors by the waiters and brought back to the starting point, to be struck on the back of the neck by hand and thrown casually on to the heap of already captured animals. No further attention was paid, the next course being about to begin. I went behind to see the rabbits. In bloody confusion some were twitching and jerking.

One Sunday morning I missed attendance at church for my father had heard that in a large grain store at the side of the railway on the road to Brighouse, there would be a ferret hunt for rats. The ferrets were brought in bags and put into a hole where rats seemed to have entered. After a while a rat would rush out, to be seized and nipped by a waiting terrier.

Across the river was a knacker's, and it was a sight not uncommon to see a flat cart with the body of a horse under a cloth except for the legs sticking out and jogging clumsily about with the jerking cart. Horses could be born, trained, worked, and finally cut up in the same small neighbourhood.

Meat products can now be bought in tins or pre-packed. Formerly the only possibility was the purchase of raw meat.. The killing was done on the spot in the village. The name 'butcher' was literally true. There was no abattoir in the district. There were no refrigerators, but the meat could pass quickly from the live animal to the table, avoiding the dangerous mysteries of the present day.

Joseph H Hird

After I went to the Grammar School in 1909 we had Wednesday afternoon as a half-holiday. I used to go shopping at the Co-op on the low road, and it was convenient to combine this duty with waiting for a cow to be driven along the road to a butcher's shop nearby.

The killing took place underneath the shop and we loitered to watch the manoeuvring of the animal down the yard and into the room. It was a venturesome task for two men. They welcomed the additional barring in by spectators. The smell of the place may have added to the bewilderment, and there was usually prolonged shouting, grunting, waving of arms, beating with sticks before the beast could be got through the doorway and have the noose thrown over its head. The rope was passed through a ring low down in the wall, by means of which the head could be drawn down close to the floor. We had a perfect view as the face was towards the open door. The butcher took a kind of hammer with a long shaft. Swinging this mightily he aimed at the forehead. The impact made the cow shudder and stagger. There was luck in the operation. On a good day the animal would drop heavily over towards the butcher's side, but at times several blows were necessary; one heard the dull crack but the cow remained on its feet. An accurate aim was difficult as the axe had to be swung through a wide arc to get the necessary violence of impact. On a bad day the blow would go dangerously near an eye. When the soft spot had been arrived at and the fittering body was down, a cane was thrust into the hole in the forehead to stir up the brain, whereupon all jerking of the legs ceased. The throat was slit and we watched the stream of frothing blood run out of the room and down the gutter by which we were standing. The interesting part of the work was now over, and we drifted away.

My father and I, when we were in Huddersfield once, walked through the slaughterhouse and saw the sheep being dealt with. They were pushed and bullied forward one at a time, and the slaughterman had a kind of wrestling match till he overpowered the sheep and got it on to its back on a trestle-table. The manoeuvre required strength and the knack. The ready, very sharp knife promptly ended any further difficulty with that one. We watched this spectacle without any enquiry as to who we were or what we wanted.

I mention another instance of drastic treatment of animals, passing over the numerous whackings of horses by bad tempered drivers. Coming into the station at Leeds (now City Station) in 1915, I saw a horse collapsed in its shafts just outside the entrance to the concourse. A man came and, after violent tugging had failed to make it rise, poured something into an ear, whereupon the horse seemed to be in two parts, the front end, up to the middle of the back, starting up, and the back part remaining unmoved. Then the animal collapsed and lay still.

Joseph H Hird

16

The River Calder and Canal

The Pennines in the north of England are somewhat to the west, and the rivers draining eastwards are rather shallow and sluggish, and not suitable for traffic throughout their length. The series of developments down our Calder Valley was: first the road alongside the river; then the river plus canal; then back again to the road with the development of motor transport.

In my time at Mirfield the steps in that progression were not clearly defined. There was still horse transport on the road, and horse plus barge on the canal, besides further ranging goods transport on the railway.

The river and canal were only about a quarter of an hour's walk from our hill. At a weir Stott's flour mill had been built. It was a terminus for a barge bringing corn from Goole. This barge was home for a family, with a cabin at each end and a chimney sticking out of one of them. A narrow walk at one side of the barge connected them, and they were quite private as access was by a hatch.

246

My Yorkshire Folk in the Early 1900s

At the side of the towpath there was a parallel depression where the hooves of the shire horse, straining against the towrope, had dug in. I saw from time to time a horse passing our house on the way down to the canal. The man sat sideways, for evidently the back of the horse was too wide for sitting astride. A large nosebag was suspended from the collar. The vast weight which one of these horses could pull showed how economical canal traffic was, where speed was not important.

Besides the grain for the flour mill, barley came to the two malt kilns. One of these, adjacent to Station Road, emitted a fragrant smell from its open windows. The floors were heated and the layer of barley was turned with very broad shovels, such as some people use for pushing snow away.

The River Calder and its canal added to the topographical interest of our district. I have realised this since leaving, not having lived within a few miles of a river since then. The water and the banks were not only interesting in themselves for short unpeopled walks and the pleasure of browsing amongst the various plants and flowers, but there was always, except on Sundays, the hope that a cart-horse would appear from the distance, digging its toes into the well-churned earth on the embankment as it strained at the bar behind. To this was fastened the stout rope from the forepart of the deck of a barge, so loaded with coal or sacks of grain that the narrow side gangways slid along only a few inches above water level.

I admired these horses pulling so willingly in the awkward angular position and requiring very little encouragement from the accompanying teamer. I think there was a kind of staging arrangement, whereby a horse and owner could be hired to meet and tow over a given section of the journey from Goole inland over the Calder and Hebble Navigation system. We frequently met, on the main road along the valley near the canal, one of the powerful horses with the towbar bumping clumsily against its back legs while the man sat up there staring lazily about and smoking a short clay pipe. The collar frame had extensions of the iron part sticking up several inches. At one side was hung an overcoat, neatly rolled, and tied with a string bend to make a loop in the middle of the coat for hanging up; on the other side, to balance, was the large nose-bag containing oats.

The anticipatory pleasure of the horses was evident when they felt the bag being attached by the loop over their heads, their impatience to get at the oats often hindering the beginning of the meal they had for several hours been working hard to deserve. As the oats diminished the horse would toss up the bag to make the remaining oats more accessible. The consequence was some spilling of the contents of the bag on the ground around the horse's head, to the delight of a small army of attendant sparrows, venturing so close that an impatient stamp sent them fluttering upwards for a moment.

The nose-bag way of feeding was not used by 'the better sort' of travellers stopping for a meal or a drink with their traps or their waggonettes. If the vehicle was small enough, the horse, still attached, was led into the shed, where oats were poured into the manger on the side of the wall. This was less wasteful than the method with nosebag and was pleasanter for the horse in rain or hot weather sunshine. These sheds were useful also for travellers on foot for shelter in a downpour.

The Battyeford stretch of waterways had quite a busy life. The Calder was joined near Cooper Bridge by the Colne coming down from Huddersfield, a tributary which had been joined by one of its own up in the Pennines, the Holme. The Calder then ran eastwards to be joined by the Spen Beck at Ravensthorpe, to lose its independence at Castleford where the Aire absorbed it.

Castleford maids must needs be fair,
They wash in the Calder and rinse in the Aire.

At the locks there was an interlude in the towing. Turning the wheel to open the heavy gates at one end for the lock to fill, watching the water rise, the entry of the barge was not easy with such weight and no one to assist. In giving the right amount of gentle movement, the sinking of the barge and the exit through the other heavy gates now slowly opening as the others had been, the re-attachment of the horse, all this was a leisurely operation worth watching. It was a reminder of the enterprise and labour of men of an earlier generation who had made it possible to transport by water heavy loads across the Pennines from one coast to the other.

On a barge during journeys between Goole and Battyeford with corn for Stott's flour mill, lived a girl of my own age. She was an intermittent member of the class at the Nab School. Her life ran in four stages: Goole to Mirfield, barge loaded, the stay at the flour mill for unloading, the return empty, the pause for re-loading, thus giving two school periods and two working holidays. She might have been expected to be rough and educationally backward. On the contrary she was quite up to the average, reticent and neat. She was not nervous but more inclined to watch than to partake in the little opportunities for free activity, and always showed economy of movement. She had been disciplined by living in a small space, the need to take care in moving, and contact with the work by which the family made its modest livelihood.

Our Sunday School superintendent, Tom Clough, worked with two sons on the canal, dredging. This work was carried out solely by muscular power. Big scoops with long shafts were lowered and dragged a little way along the bottom, then raised hand-below-hand till the scoop could be dragged over the side of the barge for emptying into the hold. Tom Clough, as might be expected, was a strong man, with huge, heavy hands. Our superintendents never took any part in the 'lessons' at Sunday School, confining their activities in the school before the journey across to church to clanging the bell, announcing the hymn, and some shouting. Two of these activities were impossible in church, where I was sent with others up into the gallery at the back till entry to the front seat with choir probationers removed me far away from Sunday school supervision. I had not been thus relieved of the boredom and consequent tendency to fidgety distractions resulting from the unintelligibility of the remote activities below and at the East End, before feeling the weight of Tom Clough's mighty hand. He came up from behind one Sunday morning and gave me such a blow on the right ear that I was dazed and felt a ringing in my head for some time.

There was another instance of Tom's rough method of child training. While he and his men were at work dredging one day, one child among a group watching and playing on the bank fell into the canal. Tom managed to reach and attach the child with the boat hook, pulled it near the barge, reached a hand down; but instead of lifting him out immediately, gave the child a good ducking first.

Mill Fires

We had multi-storey mills for woollens, cotton and blankets all near the river and canal. During my young days we lost two mills by fire. The fire at Stott's flour mill brought to an end traffic on that part of the Calder and Hebble Waterway. The mill itself was at the side of a weir where, presumably, there had been enough head of water to supply power, but in my time steam power was used. Easy to see at the side, near the water's edge, was a set of ropes on huge pulleys, and I did not fail to go and watch them whenever I went down to the canal bank. On the land side all the wooden structure and the yard adjacent were white with flour.

The fire at Stott's mill happened during a school holiday at a time when I was on my own at home. My parents had gone to work, my father to the pit, my mother to her loom at Learoyd's. I was asleep, when I was wakened by the sound of people running down the hill past the house. I got up and went out and found the cause. I was down at the riverside very quickly. The fire engine was roaring, drawing water from the river to send up in jets. All the attack on the conflagration was from the ground, as the fire engine had no crane or ladders. There was no fire service in Mirfield.

Nothing could be done to resist the spread of fire until the arrival of horses from Huddersfield or Dewsbury, pulling the heavy pump driven by steam heated with coal and carrying the crew of helmeted firemen with hatchet in belt. The horses were still giving off a cloud of vapour after their rush to the scene. There were so many spectators that we had to take care not to slip into the river, and the firemen yelled to us not to hinder. As a spectacle only one thing was lacking in this great blaze, so quickly consuming all that dry woodwork: it happened in daylight.

This was not so with the other fire at Crowther's, a textile mill a little further down the river. It took place in the evening, and this time my father hurried down with me. The weather was fine and dark. There were several storeys and we watched all the mill windows full of blaze and the melted glass running down. At intervals there was a great thud as a floor collapsed under the weight of machinery and sent skyward a cloud of flame and black objects. Some of us ventured down the yard round the side, getting wet by standing inadvertently in little jets of water shooting out from pinpricks in the hoses. The firemen wanted more room. One of them suddenly started running, shouting, "Boilers! Boilers!". The yard was clear in a few seconds.

The loss of these two mills reduced the workaday chorus of sirens (hooters) calling the workers at six o'clock in the morning. The sirens were not synchronised, and went off in sequence, as if one attentive night watchman had noticed the time and reminded the others. For railwaymen there was the 'knocker-up' system with a man visiting particular houses with his knocker on a pole.

The sirens were a not unpleasant disturbance of the silence, but were to become anachronistic when most workmen would be able to afford a watch. A watch, however, was still a heavy inconvenient object, needing the security of a chain. It was more suitable for slinging across a waistcoat from one pocket to the other, with a little bar for suspension in the middle and, in my father's case, an 'Albert' (medal) to anchor in the opposite pocket. For working men a watch was a weekend accessory. In those days I never saw a wrist watch.

Church bells were also a historical reminder of the days before workers carried watches, but the sounds went back a long time before the Industrial Revolution. Also the ringing on Sundays may have had a special urgency when attendance at church was ordered by the law. Church bells also announced disasters and political uprisings.

Boat-building

Near the centre of Mirfield the canal and the river are at a considerable distance from each other, the canal being near the main road down Newgate and Mirfield (Lancashire and Yorkshire) Railway Station. Not only did barges visit Mirfield: they were built there. Originally there were two boatyards, one of them in Battyefor but the more important, and surviving, one was near Mirfield station. On my journeys thither I could follow the repairs in the dry dock and the progress of building a new barge on the stocks. Progress could easily be seen day by day, so we knew when at last the day would come for the launching, a delicate operation against the narrow canal. This took place broadside, there being not enough room for a fore-and-aft slipway. The launch was a fine sight, with the booming 'plomp' into the canal, the huge wash swilling up the banks and the wobble of the barge till it gradually got its balance. But it went off perfectly.

With the coming of modern road traffic, canal and river transport diminished, though it continued for long to have a use in the supply of coal, of which a large quantity could be moved in one journey and with little use of machinery. It was an advantage that the man engaged in this kind of traffic could live on his vehicle with his family.

There has been some return to the waterway recently for pleasure travel, and a few years ago a barge was fitted out for trips by the authority, now under the Government. We went on one of these trips, joining a coach at the Alhambra in Bradford. It was a 'mystery' excursion. We were taken to Dewsbury, where we went down into a barge for the voyage which ended in Wakefield, where there was another coach journey for the return to Bradford. The bottom of the barge had been fitted as a cabin with seats athwart and windows for sightseeing, with a hood in case of rain. There was a little refreshment bar, and a small lavatory with a handle to pump instead of chain. The scenery was not very attractive; it was familiar to me.

The man at the wheel, which was one like that on ships with the hand grips round the circumference, was inexpert and at times bumped one bank and corrected the error by over-compensating and bumping the opposite bank. The women in the party shrieked with excitement at this, but there was some discussion amongst us men as to whether the old barge would survive the treatment.

The captain of the boat had an engineer as assistant with the power supply, but though communication between them was immediate, and they were obviously keen about the performance, the passage through locks was an adventure, with some bumping and shuddering. The sinking down in the lock to get to the lower level for the exit was interesting, and disgusting. Little fountains gushed out from the cracks in the stone wall sides against the windows, and the walls themselves were covered with filthy slime. The stench, increasing as we sank, made it evident that there was much room for improvement in the purification systems in the upper reaches of the Calder

The 'Ha'p'ni' (Halfpenny) Bridge across the Calder was a structure erected by private enterprise as a toll bridge. At a gate in front of a small hut, one paid the ½d toll at the window. The few people living on the south side had an arrangement for a weekly payment to cover all their necessary crossings, for there were no shops over there, only farming and the day-hole mine. Apart from this bridge, there was no crossing for about two miles in each direction.

It may have been possible hereabouts to ford the rivers as it is shallow and stony a short distance above the present bridge, but in times of heavy rain there can have been little communication between the few habitations on the southern side and the more populous area along the main road through the valley. Building of houses on the steep scar on the north side of the river had been much more difficult than it would have been on the south, but the advantage had been the main road on the north side and the growth of industry.

Annie's parents could remember examples of 'spite and malice' houses. These were erected on remains of common land not yet appearing on plans, but likely to be an unwelcome intrusion on the amenities of nearby residents. The house might be little more than a shed, but if erected and with smoke rising within the twenty-four hours, it could stand.

In time the need to be able to cross the river at this place grew. Easier access to the textile mills and to shops was required, and a regular, safe way of crossing the water had to be found and the bridge was built.

In the last years of my parents' time at Kitson Hill, a farmer called Fred Archer used to come on a certain evening in mid-week to fetch a clothes basketful of my mother's newly baked bread. His farm was on the south side. It had been Ellam's farm in my boyhood and we had been able from the playground at the Nab School to look across and watch the seasonal activities on the slope opposite ours. Our interest was stimulated by John Arthur Popplewell, a classmate whose father worked across there and who himself accompanied the horses in his spare time. Fred Archer had succeeded to the farm, where he had spent the whole of his life. He had never had any other interest, except chapel (Primitive Methodist) on Sunday, being so strict in observance that he would never work in the field on Sunday, even if he might by doing so have saved a crop of corn from a soaking.

Fred was now an elderly man and used to sit for a while on the chair near the door, a slow exchange of gossip going on while my mother packed into the clothes basket the teacakes which had been set up on end on the breadboard. Fred was to carry the basket on his head down the hill and across the Halfpenny Bridge. He never had any other cereal food than my mother's teacakes.

He happened to speak of the Nab School once when I was at Kitson Hill on baking night. He knew about Battye who, before the bridge was built, would cross the river as a ferryman when called for. Fred had attended the Nab school, and the transport of children who lived over the water gave regular work for Battye on school days. The hours were convenient, coming after the workers' time in the morning and before in the evening. Battye was strict with the children. They had to get there together and promptly after school, or he would punish a latecomer by making him wait on the wrong side.

Near the bridge which replaced the ferry there is still a gap in the wall adjoining the main road from which steps lead steeply down to the water where the boat could come close in.

Although it may have been possible to ford the river upstream by riding across on horseback or a cart, or even by wading, that had been abandoned. The name 'ford', nevertheless, came to be associated with Mr Battye. Now 'Battye's ford' has become Battyeford, and applies to an area far beyond the original spot.

The local inhabitants retained the significance of the name by pronouncing the stress on *ford*. Strangers, like the Resurrection monks, annoyed me by pronouncing the name as *Battyefud*.

17

My Parents in Retirement

My mother continued to weave for about twenty years after I left Mirfield, but gave up after my father stopped working. There were coincidences here. In 1921 or thereabouts, certainly after September of that year, the Three Nuns Pit stopped. The seams were not thick and the coalface was becoming more and more remote. While I was at home my father used to refer to the long journeys underground mentioning, for example, under the New Inn at Hartshead up to two miles away. He was transferred to the next less remote of the Low Moor chain of pits at Hartshead. He was familiar with the place, having gone there on occasion for overtime repair work, with a consequent long walk for me up the company's waggon road with a meal for him.

At the age of fifty he was tired by the time he had walked from Kitson Hill to Hartshead. He was always impeded by the amount of excessive weight he carried, due

259

mainly to the large amount of bread eaten. I suggested that he might cycle, and persuaded him to try on my machine, but he was so clumsy that the experiment quickly ended. His diet also led to bowel trouble, and he stopped working. My mother ended her long career at the loom. She was about forty-eight years of age.

A new regime started. Recovering from the indisposition which had been the cause of his retirement, my father had leisure to assess his situation. His 'speculation' in me had been a disappointment, but his savings and investments had given him confidence. His 'ship had come home'. Detachment from pit concerns had a beneficial effect. There was no further material for the nightly cursing and grumbling about work. He sought distraction in gossip with other retired working men whom he met on their walks up our hill. A seat overlooking the scene southwards across to the hillside over the Calder became like a little open-air club on a pleasant summer's afternoon. The objective interest of sport made for safe conversation. It was a surprise to me in the twenties and thirties how interested my father could be in the progress of Huddersfield Town. In my youth he had despised footballers as 'flannelled fools'. Now he even went out to the gate to call out to men coming up the hill on their return from watching, in order to get results and comments. (Ease of travel and the higher standards expected by spectators had caused the local teams to fade out.) In summer he went to Park Avenue in Bradford to watch county matches.

This way of coming out of himself was a very good thing. Without ever forgiving me, he acquiesced in the inevitable about me.

My Yorkshire Folk in the Early 1900s

Grandchildren to see from time to time, and Annie's understanding of him and her way with my mother brought some warmth into his heart, and we were even able to take them camping with us. On one of these occasions, for example, at Hest Bank, Morecambe, we had twelve people in our tent when a gale blew down a neighbour's tent. Yet, even in such crowding, my father was at ease, smoking his pipe and playing a game with Annie.

Improvements in travel helped in broadening outlook. In my boyhood my mother's range was: mill, house, weekend local Co-op. For this journey she wore the usual big shawl, a convenient garment. Folded diagonally, it was easily put over the head to frame the face and fasten with a blanket safety-pin, always ready in place to link across under the chin. The shawl covered all down to below the waist, so there was no need to 'put soomat on' when going out. In the Co-op the part over the head was pushed back on the shoulder till it was time to leave. When wider shopping became possible that would not do. Women began to meet other women than the few they had known from childhood and felt a need to 'look decent'.

A Friday market started in Mirfield in front of the Black Bull and women began to catch the little bus which passed the bottom of Kitson Hill. They could, by the same means, get to Huddersfield or Dewsbury. My parents began a habit of going to a cinema at Ravensthorpe, walking at first, then becoming more fastidious about the films and catching a bus to go the Playhouse at Dewsbury.

These things led to a change and social ease which seemed to me wonderful. The house I had known, rarely entered by a fourth person, became quite a 'call 'oil', my mother's small-scale grocery sales being a pretext for frequent calls and exchange of local information.

There were limits, however, to their facility in communication. In travel, my parents never arranged a journey for themselves beyond a rare half-day excursion, or a booking with a holiday agency.

Neither of them ever used a telephone. My mother came over to Bradford to see my grandmother Brown when word came that she was failing. Return home that night was intended, but my grandmother was so far gone that my mother's continued presence was necessary. Worried about my father not knowing why if she did not come home that night, she rushed back to Mirfield to tell him, and rushed back to Bradford, almost collapsing with exhaustion. I asked her why she did not send a telegram. Such a possibility had not occurred to her.

Curious things were done about diet. Someone said that onions were good for the bowels. Accordingly, large quantities were bought and boiled. Meat came under suspicion, but was thought essential for strength. Plenty of meat was bought but none eaten, only the gravy being consumed. This diet was modified by changing the meaning of *meat*. This word now meant beef, so there was a change to mutton, which was not meat. Wisely, more fruit was eaten, of which there had never been enough in my time. That my father (and indeed to a lesser extent my mother too) was too fat was not discussed. He weighed over eleven stone and, for his height, he ought not to have weighed more than nine stone.

My mother continued her gainful activity. She went out part-time charring for better-off neighbours; she baked for the farmer, Fred Archer, and she sold groceries and oddments of household requisites to neighbours who called to make a small purchase and to gossip. The small profit on these transactions was obtained by having bulk delivery from the Co-op cart and getting the dividend, customers buying at shop price but getting no dividend.

In connection with this period of my parents' life a modification of attitude towards economics should be mentioned. From earlier than I can remember my father had made monthly journeys on Saturdays to Huddersfield to keep up with the half-crown share subscriptions in the Huddersfield Building Society. In time he had enough money to buy some shares in the Yorkshire Electric Power Company, whose plant at Thornhill, near Dewsbury, he could watch growing. He also put a little money into oil (BP) and railways, as well as Consols. This nest egg which he was building up gave him more confidence (and a great deal of pride and subject for meditation over prospectuses and reports and vouchers) and changed him from the pro-Labour and anti-boss attitude prevalent among the workers to an awareness of the importance of capital and management.

He kept in firm command of the capital, allowing my mother to have only a much smaller sum than himself. Indeed, he thought that what

---

she had should be under his control. On one occasion, after it had become necessary to have a bank account (Martin's Bank, Huddersfield) a cheque was held up. It was for my mother but he had signed her name.

With the exception of the month after my birth and the period following our removal to Mirfield, ie from April to January 1901 when I was sent out to lodge, my mother had spent as long a time going out to work and had had a longer day, with her evening work to follow, but it was my father's policy to prevent her from acquiring financial independence. He stopped her capital at £800.

After the recovery of his health my father entered upon his last period, the fifteen years up to his death in 1937. Wireless came in and when, with the improvement of sets, he wished to change from wet batteries to mains current, he paid for the installation of electricity himself. Incidentally he had a curious mishap when discussing the position for a light upstairs. The electrician had taken up floor-boards and in the discussion my father stepped back; my mother downstairs was suddenly alarmed with a shower of plaster and the sight of my father's leg descending.

The chief sign of 'the ship having come home' was the commencement of holidays. There had been none while I was at home but now, each summer, there was a week at Blackpool and a holiday by coach with a Lancashire firm, Pleasureways.

With regard to his shares, as the Yorkshire Electric Power Company developed, my father was given some rights, accruing from the investments he had made. He told me he would not let me have these (and, of course, my mother had not to be allowed to acquire more capital). So he went to Clifton, near Brighouse, to give them to a former pitman, Joseph Tattersall ('Jooa Tatt') whom he met at times to discuss former days. He advised me, however, to get some shares in the open market, which I did to please him.

My father decided not to allow himself to increase his income. He wished to avoid paying income tax. With my mother's supplementary efforts, and the moderate indulgence of the holidays, a weekly walk to a cinema and a more lavish table, my father considered that they were comfortable. Time has shown however that, nationalised, his investments are worth far less than he thought, and that the National Retirement Pension for one person is far higher than the interest from the capital built up over a long period of hard work, and which he thought adequate for the two of them to live in comfort.

The course of my career had led to disappointment. My father felt a kind of ownership over both my mother and me. From the time of the County Minor Scholarship when I was eleven, he had regarded me as a speculation, an investment, the price being that I was to be allowed to spend several years bringing in no wage, and getting through my time without "ever doing an hour's work".

In fact, his sacrifice for my maintenance was slight. We had an extremely simple way of living. At about fifteen years of age I received a West Riding County Council Bursarship (implying an intention to enter upon a teaching career and a willingness to serve for at least two years in the West Riding). At eighteen I had my first paid post as a teacher. While away in the Navy during the War I sent home five shillings a week and on my return my war-service grant made me self-supporting.

In my teens my father had shown what his plan for me was. I was to qualify, get a post, live at home, hand over my salary and get spending money. This routine was to continue for a long time.

Interest in the opposite sex was going to be tolerated. As I have mentioned, my mother had made practical suggestions about this. There was a model for my probable sentimental relationship. One of the women who walked from the tram at Bradley with my mother had a 'chap'. This man came to their house every evening and sat, often falling asleep, while the woman went on with her housework. This routine lasted till they were forty and got married. Had I followed the same way, my father's scheme would have been admirably fulfilled. He died six weeks before I was forty.

My Yorkshire Folk in the Early 1900s

The failure of his investment in me brought about much grumbling over my ingratitude. Soon after I began working in Bradford my father had an absence from work because of the first signs of his bowel trouble. I offered to pay him £2 a week if he would stop working. He refused it, but did not stop grumbling. A reckoning was made of what I had cost in maintenance from the time when I might have left the Elementary School to start working. My father had received money from my Bursarship, my teaching posts before and after war service, the grant I had made out of service pay (the five shillings came with two shillings and sixpence added by the Government), the West Riding Studentship granted for my Division 1 result in the Matriculation Examination, and I was self-supporting on the war service grant to students. When all these were allowed for, the amount for my maintenance came to £103. My father was offered this and again refused.

He died on the 25th of November 1937. During his strolls he had noticed that other retired men were interested in football matches between teams of local lads. In order to be able to understand their criticisms of the play, he began to go to a field where the teams played. November was wet and he stood in wet grass during the match. His footwear was not expertly mended (my father mended his boots with bucket leather brought home from work; the leather had been discarded at the pit and was somewhat denatured). So, on that November afternoon my father's feet were soaked. He caught cold, but took no particular precautions. He even carried on with a repair to the wall of the coalplace and, of course, had to take the usual walk round the two houses and along the garden at the back to reach the closet.

Thursday came, baking day as usual. This time my father prolonged his afternoon nap in bed upstairs. His chest was causing trouble. My mother became worried, so much so that she went to the currier's mill a few yards away and asked if there was some way of letting me know in Bradford, where I was teaching at Carlton School. Telephones were not allowed in schools at that time, and our neighbour telephoned Bradford Technical College and got a message to me. I ran home to Lidget Green, got the car out and sped to Mirfield.

My mother was saying a few words to me as I entered, when my father called out: "Mary, I'm chokin'!". We went upstairs in time to see him sit up, with eyes protruding, and then fall back, dead. He had not understood that he had caught pneumonia and it had filled his lungs.

That happened in the middle of the baking, and there was an ovenful of bread. In spite of the emergency, my mother came down and got that bread out at the right moment, in the usual perfect condition.

My Yorkshire Folk in the Early 1900s

My mother spent on his grave at Mirfield Parish Church the total sum of the 10 shillings a week pension which he had been drawing between his 65th birthday and his death: it was £50. The grave has now disappeared.

My father's heart was never in the least softened towards me. Also the only occasion when my mother was at all moved in her attitude to me was when I was with her in 1944 during the last days of the (breast) cancer from which she had been suffering for several months and treating with poultices. She said: "You've done very well."

Both my father and mother had been brought up in families where there was no expression of affection. On those rare occasions when we went to Low Moor or Bowling to see relatives, the motive was curiosity after the passage of time rather than any inclination to show warmth. Reared in the ambience of mutual indifference, I acquired a permanent dislike of expressions of tenderness, as 'sloppy'.

Joseph H Hird

Hirds from Elizabeth I to Elizabeth II

Although Joe felt the ancestry he wrote about in his memoirs here had breadth but little depth, he was later able to remedy this through a contact made in the USA, Edward Hird. Edward had been tracing his descent from a Yorkshire ancestor, and contacted Joe when he read an article in the Bradford Telegraph and Argus. It described a reunion of sailors from WW1 which included Joe.

1546-1636 **John Hird**=m 1573 Anne Claypham

1574-1623 **Christopher Hird**=m 1600 Elizabeth Smythe

1617-1672 **William Hird**=m (1) 1645 Mary Hall; =m(2)1650 Martha Whittikers

1652-? **John Hird**=m 1678 Sarah Cordingley

1678-? **William Hird**=m 1702

1703-? **Thomas Hird**=m 1729 Mercy Waterhouse

1731-? **Joseph Hird**=m 1753 Ann Driver

1767-1822 **Joseph Hird**=m (1);=m (2) Mary Sharpe

1798-1842 **Joseph Hird**=m 1822 Rose Anna Town

1834-1880 **John Hird** =m 1855 Harriet Horrocks 1835-1892

1870-1937 **Samuel Hird**=m 1897 Mary Brown 1874-1944

1898-1990 **Joseph Henry Hird**=m 1922 Annie Bottomley 1897-1985

1928- **Brian Hird**=m1953 Barbara Nicholson 1928-

Compiled by Edward Hird, New Jersey USA, 1982

Joseph H Hird

Glossary

barcelonas	Spanish hazel nuts
bend	knot to fasten a rope to a ring
bobbin-ligging	pegging spools of thread on a railing: a basic job given to new mill workers
brat	overall or apron
charabanc	long horse-drawn open carriage for excursions, later motorised
cheque	metal token used by the Co-op as a record of purchases qualifying for dividend
chumping	West Riding term for gathering fuel for Bonfire Night
collops	cooked sliced food, often potatoes
corve	pit wagon
cratch	wooden chair with semi-circular arms and back rest connecting to the seat with bars
currier	specialist in dyeing and processing leather
datler	mine-worker responsible for clearing shale
day-hole	shallow mine with surface entrance
felling out	finishing weaving a long stretch of worsted cloth
felloe	the part of the rim of a wooden wheel where spokes are inserted
fettler	cleaning man in the mills
flag	large flat level stone
gas mantle	fabric covering for a gas flame impregnated with metal nitrates to give a white light
havercake	pancake made of oats and water, baked without fat on a hot stove

hurrier	miner's boy assistant
Irish moss	seaweed, used to clarify beer and make jelly
laiking	playing, idling
maul	large hammer
midden	dung and waste heap
mistral	cow shed
nessy	outdoor dry closet
one-decker	single-storey house with low attic
overlooker	overseer
peggy	wooden device like a stool with a rod, used during washing
poke	cloth bag for carrying flour etc
pomatum	pomade, a waxy greasy substance to keep hair slick and shiny
posnet	large three-legged pan for boiling clothes
posser	large copper cup on a shaft for moving clothes up and down during washing
puddler	stirrer of molten iron to separate out impurities
ruddle	yellow ocherous stone used for rubbing on doorsteps and window sills
sitting up	attending a communal outdoor event on a tiered platform
skep	large round basket
skid	iron shoe to increase drag when a cart was going down a hill
teamer	haulier
tenter	wooden frame on which to stretch large pieces of cloth held tight by hooked nails
thible	pudding stick
tram	pit wagon without sides

Acknowledgements and thanks

Kirklees Library: permission to reproduce parts of *Mirfield: Life in a West Riding Village, 1900-1914* by Joseph H Hird, 1983

Huddersfield Council Libraries: photos from *Mirfield: Life in a West Riding Village, 1900-1914* by Joseph H Hird, 1983

Family photographs courtesy of Bessie Walshaw (neé Hird) and her estate

Corrie Lesser: Joe in a school collar

DanielCRMirfield: photos of House of Resurrection

HaroldFB Wheeler: motor charabanc, 1921

Mary Bowles (neé Hird): proofreading

National Archives UK: Trevor Huddlestone

Philip Cooley: sketch of horse and cart

RedSimon: Jowett tourer

Typ932: Morgan 3-wheeler

Wikipedia

Printed in Great Britain
by Amazon.co.uk, Ltd.,
Marston Gate.